With every best Wish

'Frank's bench'

The true story of
A boy, A Ship with a secret, and a
WW2 German POW camp.

'A grave mistake, or a Churchill Conspiracy'

Captain Peter Thomson

Copyright © Peter Thomson (2023)

The right of Peter Thomson to be identified as the author of this work has been asserted by him in accordance with the Copyright, Design and Patents Act (1988)

This is a true account where the factual material has been obtained by interview and research and tested as far as is possible by the author for veracity. Where opinions are expressed to fill factual gaps these are those of the author who has taken every endeavour to cover any factual omission as an unbiased supposition. Where the author's expressed opinions are proven to be inaccurate, the author undertakes to correct the text forthwith and to apologise for any offense the said suppositions or opinions might have caused.

It is the author's stated objective for 'Frank's bench' to deliver an accurate portrayal of the life and times of Frank William Walker.

All rights reserved. No part of this publication may be reproduced, stored in a retrieval system, or transmitted in any form, or by any means, electronic, mechanical, photocopying, recording or otherwise without the prior permission of the author, save for the purpose of posting an honest review.

Cover design by Cats Pyjamas Design
(catspyjamasdesign.com)

Front Cover: Image: Reproduced from a British government poster of World War 2 under licence from the Science Museum, London.

Rear Cover Image: Mrs. Vera Walker sitting on Frank's bench. Photograph reproduced courtesy of Nautilus Care and Welfare board

❧ Created with Vellum

DEDICATION

This biography is dedicated to the memory of the crewmen who died aboard the *S.S. Automedon* on the 11th November 1940 as a consequence of German surface raider Atlantis's shellfire.

William Brown Ewan,
Peter Lindsay Whittaker
William Gordon Diggle
James Joseph Watts
Percy John Mosely
Thomas Geoffrey Wilson

And also:
Guardsman 2697562 Gilbert McKeand, 2nd Bn. Scot's Guards
Who gave his life on the mined road to Milag-Marlag Nord camp to bring freedom to its inmates on 26th April 1945

'In the halls of heroes their names shall ring out for freedom for evermore'

'Merchant Navy Association'

From ship to shore, from past to present

The Wirral Branch of the Merchant Navy Association is proud to be associated with this important historical record of a young British seafarer and of his fellow civilian seamen taken by force into captivity when the country was at war.

Lest We Forget!
*

Chairman: Mr. Arthur Speed

Hon. Secretary: Mr. Bernard Smith

Treasurer Mr. Robert Keith

"Old and Young we are all on our last cruise!"
Robert Louis Stevenson

'A Season in Hell'

Arthur Rimbaud (1873)

⚜

My eternal soul,
Redeem your vow.
In spite of the lonely night
And the day on fire!

⚜

Mon âme éternelle

Observe ton voeu.

Malgré la nuit seule

Et le jour en feu!

⚜

'COME ON LADS WE ARE GOING TO FIGHT!'

An Historical Dissertation
by
Captain Peter Thomson

'Pinguin's' attack on S.S. Maimoa, November, 1940 Painting by Les Cowle, Courtesy of Dunshea89.wixsite.com/dunshea-escapes1941

FOREWORD:

Sometimes in history the largest events turn on the smallest of issues. Often these unpredictable events culminate in catastrophic consequences that academics broadly describe as *'Black Swan'* moments.

The event that befell the world, and the man whose memory this book honours while he was only sixteen years of age, and serving on his first trip to sea as a deck boy in 1940, must rank as the blackest swan moment of all time.

If at 07:58 local time on 11th November 1940, Frank William Walker's captain on the Blue Funnel liner *'Automedon'* had not allowed his ship to close with the German surface raider *Atlantis* in the Indian Ocean , Japan might not have attacked the American fleet in Pearl Harbour on the 7th December 1941–or even at all.

The outcome of this misfortune for Frank and his shipmates rendered them directly, but unknowingly responsible for turning what had until then been a purely European conflict into the Second World War. This book will explain that controversial statement during the telling of Frank Walker's story.

So who was Frank Walker?

His story begins on the west bank of the River Mersey in the sleepy dormitory town of Wallasey, where close to the old main entrance gate to Mariners' Park stands a memorial bench that bears a small brass plate engraved with a simple inscription: 'Frank's Bench' and below it, the years '1924 -2008'.

We learn from the inscription that Frank lived for 84 years, but it says nothing at all about the man, or his life. I never knew Frank in person, but I did learn of him through accepting the tacit challenge the twin lines of that caption on his memorial bench threw at me: a challenge to learn more about him. Thus stimulated, I set out to research his life. My findings about Frank Walker, of the *Automedon* and his fellow seafarers, and how they lived through their extraordinary trials, tribulations and adventures follow.

Captain Peter Thomson,

WALLASEY,

April 2023.

Your Girl's Gonna Love a
DICKIN'S
CIDER
GIVE HER ONE
TODAY
IN THE
DOCKYARD
CANTEEN !
ONLY 2' 6d
HM SUBS AND SHIPS ON

FRANK'S EARLY LIFE:

'Frank's Bench and his wife, Vera' *Photo courtesy of Danny Kenny of Nautilus International.*

* * *

I made a regular habit of pausing to sit on Frank's Bench on my return walks from shopping forays, just for a few minutes. On these occasions I would thank him for his bench being in exactly the right position when I needed it there to afford me a little rest on my returns to our new home at the Mariners' Park. In that way I became acquainted with him. So, who was the real Frank Walker?

There is little readily available information about Frank and his early life, but after research, and with the help of his lovely wife Vera and others who knew him—the story that follows is the result of these inquiries.

'Frank William Walker,' Aged 16 *Photo courtesy of Mrs. Vera Walker.*

Francis William Walker was born into modest circumstances at Rusholme, Manchester on 22nd August 1924. He then lived with his parents on Merseyside in rented accommodation close to King Street in Wallasey and within a mile of where Frank would live in peaceful retirement until he passed away in 2008.

As a boy he suffered an unhappy childhood, for he could do nothing right for his father, who took every opportunity to lay his hands heavily upon the lad.

He regularly witnessed his parents at loggerheads with each other. On most days whenever the two came together, Frank would find them engaged in a vicious argument. These domestic rows continued for what seemed like hours with neither his mother nor father yielding to the other. Their quarrels only came to an end when his father inflicted physical violence on his mother: violent behaviour that inevitably spilled over onto Frank, should he be unwise enough to have remained nearby while their tempers clashed.

Frank's original Merchant Navy discharge book records his height at four feet four inches (4'4"). His smallness in physical stature attracted the attention of bullies at school, who gave him the nicknames of 'Winkle' and 'Titch': handles that stayed with him for the remainder of his life.

In spite of his small physique, Frank grew up into being nobody's pushover. The daily hardships he endured strengthened his character and inner resolve to improve his lot in life.

Although he enjoyed a loving home relationship with his mother, the converse proved true for the times when he had no other choice but to associate with his father: those occasions being frequently punctuated with verbal abuse, 'clipped ears' and even more aggressive beatings.

Frank nevertheless developed a fun loving and genial nature, punctuated with a sharp wit that endeared him to his peers.

The lack of sufficient money to provide for the commonplace needs of the family, added to the tensions in the home.

About the time of his eleventh birthday, all of his schoolmates had bicycles. Not having one of his own had left Frank outside of their two-wheeled outings. He pleaded with his mother for what in his heart he knew was the impossible:

"Mum, can I have a bike? All my mates have got one."

To his delight and great surprise she said: "If you pass the eleven plus exam, you can have a bike."

"Wow! Do you promise?"

"Yes!" She replied.

Frank worked hard and he did pass the scholarship to go on to continue his education at a grammar school, but his academic triumph coincided with the total collapse of the family home. Without a word, Frank's father had disappeared, never to be heard of again, thus bringing a new start, but with different hardships for Frank and his mother to endure. Only a short time later, his mother found that she could no longer keep them both and pay the rent out of her own meagre income. In consequence, they had to move out of the home where they were living. In effect, they became homeless. His mother sought to find live-in work for herself but found she couldn't take Frank in with her to any of the appointments that opened to her. Until she could find a double-berth appointment that would allow them to live together again he had to go into care with the Sisters of Mercy in their convent in Yew Tree Lane, Liverpool.

***

Inside that bleak Pugin designed monastic masonry Frank found himself alone with: no bike; no Dad; no Mum, no home and no prospects. Life with the nuns proved to be not too dissimilar to the times when he had lived with his father. He couldn't do anything right for the holy women either. He frequently endured their tongue-lashings and corporal punishments for what he considered were no more than minor indiscretions or infractions of their rules. Frank hated it there. He badly needed a home with his mother, but he remained out of direct contact with her while she continued to be without a permanent address.

Occasional respites from the harsh and unloving regime of the Sisters occurred when a distant aunt would call to take him to her home in Sale for weekends. It provided a form of escape for him, although these days out happened only rarely.

The Sisters of Mercy also ran a school for girls on their premises. Being a boy meant that Frank could not attend the same classes as the girls. He became obliged, therefore, to seek to further his education a little farther along Yew Tree Lane. His family and friends believed that he had attended St. Vincent's School. An establishment built by the Daughters of Charity as a school for the blind in the late 1800's, and situated almost next door to the Sisters of Mercy convent. The area had earned itself the local epithet of Popes Corner, owing to the close proximity of the old Convent, St. Vincent's, Broughton Hall and Cardinal Heenan schools.

It is most likely that Frank attended one of the schools other than St. Vincent's, for he was not visually impaired. Applicants, then and now, are prohibited entry into the Merchant Navy's deck department should they suffer from imperfect eyesight. In spite of this doubt, it is worth mentioning St. Vincent's in this talk, if only to applaud the establishment for the wonderful work its staff continue to carry out today for children and others who suffer visual and sensory impairment.

Frank got on well enough with the work and with his fellow pupils at the school, but it bothered him considerably to have to spend so much time on his own–especially in the evenings. Every day that came and passed he hoped to receive a forwarding address for his mum, thus bringing with it the prospect of their renewed togetherness in a family home.

As the days became years, this hope gradually withered away. In its stead Frank began counting the days until his fourteenth birthday.

Once he had turned fourteen, he could legally leave school to fend for himself: and more especially, to be free from the place and hardships of where fate had billeted him. The emergence of that comforting thought arrived with a flood of questions in its wake, all of which gave Frank a short, sharp shock.

'Where will I live?' 'What can I do to provide for myself?' 'Who'll be there for me if I get in trouble'? 'How will I even manage to survive on my own?'

The answers to those questions lay all around him on busy Merseyside, and in every direction in which he cared to gaze out upon the river.

Frank decided he would join the Merchant Navy and go to sea, where everything would be provided for him and his needs.

St. Vincent's School, Yew Tree Lane, Liverpool. *Photo courtesy of the Principal, St. Vincent's School, Liverpool.*

World War Two Poster. *Reproduced by kind permission of the Science Museum, London.*

LEAVING SCHOOL /CANADIAN PACIFIC RAILWAY:

WILLS'S CIGARETTES
S.S. "DUCHESS OF RICHMOND"

Photo source: Flickr Maritime Cards & Boats © *All Rights Reserved.*

That great day finally arrived. On August 22nd 1938, Frank turned fourteen and reached the obligatory school leaving age of those times in England. The boy made haste in making the acquaintance of the Canadian Pacific Steamship personnel in their office in the Liver Building at the Pier Head in Liverpool; and on the 19th May 1939 he went to sea as a bellboy on their transatlantic liner, *'Duchess of Richmond'*.

Frank enjoyed his life at sea, working among the passengers delivering Canadian Pacific's Railway's hotel services on voyages to Canada. His Discharge 'A' book became a treasured possession, for it defined him as a legitimate seafarer, a man of position, one earning his own livelihood– notwithstanding, he was only fourteen years of age.

* * *

A Discharge 'A' Book, is a seaman's personal record of service at sea in the British Merchant Navy.

The first page of his Discharge book reveals an interesting feature of the early days of the Second World War.

During the First World War, genteel ladies would roam the streets of the nation seeking out men folk of military age who were not wearing the King's uniform. They would attempt to shame such males as they found into joining up by adorning them with a white feather of cowardice.

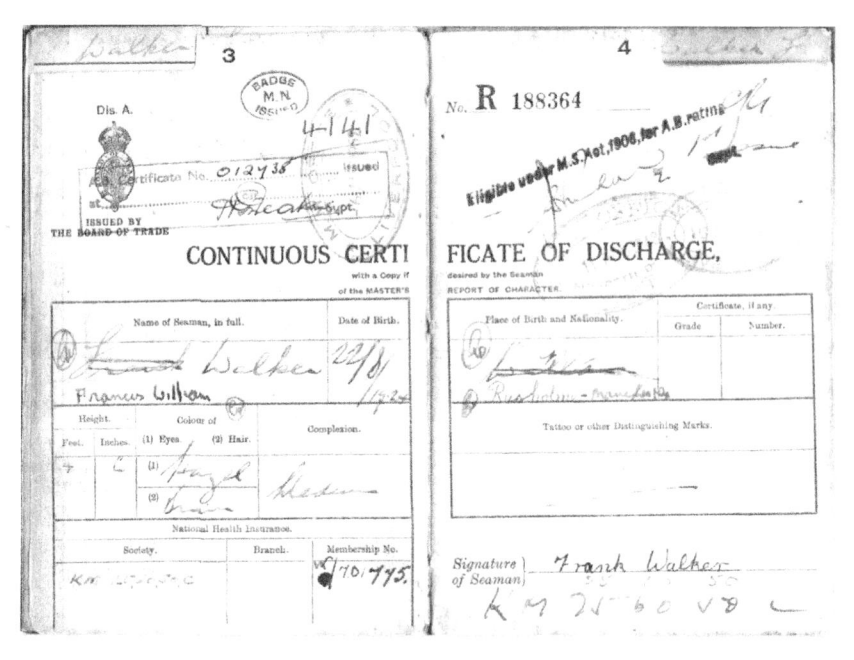

First page of Frank Walker's Discharge Book. *Reproduced by kind permission of Mrs. Vera Walker.*

Although the war drums were already beating in the summer of 1939, the war had not yet started, and these ladies were already seen to be active on city streets throughout the land.

They competed for prey with recruiters from the three regular armed services. Military scouts who were employed to prowl the thoroughfares and public houses frequented by seamen ashore, seeking out men of serviceable age to entice them into military uniforms.

Merchant seamen have always been civilians who wear plain clothes at work and ashore. Officers and some ratings do wear a form of dress, but this is a civilian livery, and not a military style of uniform. These men were, however, more precious to the nation crewing a ship at sea than in toting a rifle in the trenches of a new Flanders.

To protect seamen from the zeal of these unofficial female recruiters, and to ensure valuable seafarers were not pressed into joining the Armed services, the Department of Transport devised a badge of National Service. This to be worn by seafarers when walking ashore dressed in their usual civilian clothes.

This small bright insignia, worn in their coat lapels provided them with a shield of protection from harassment by zealous recruiters: and the manpower of the merchant fleet from their losses by enrolment into other services.

The Royal Mint struck these lapel badges in sterling silver in the now traditional Merchant Navy design. Although the badges are not numbered, each was individually issued and registered as such in a seafarer's Discharge book at the seaman's local Mercantile Marine Office: the record of issue thus being numbered rather than the actual badge issued to a man.

The issue of Frank's badge is entered into his Discharge book and numbered 4141. This is a picture of the actual badge issued to Frank in 1940.

These badges can be distinguished from the more modern castings by the horseshoe shaped lapel fastener, and also by their tendency to tarnish.

According to Gabe Thomas, an ex-Registrar of Shipping and Seamen, there were 144,000 Merchant Seamen serving aboard British vessels at the outbreak of war. This number increased to 185,000 as the war progressed.

Frank's National Service Lapel badge *Courtesy Mrs. Vera Walker.*

* * *

But we have moved a little ahead of ourselves. Let us rejoin Frank celebrating his fifteenth birthday while serving aboard the *Duchess of Richmond* in Honolulu, and while the world still remained at a fragile peace.

Of the many exotic places Frank visited on that last peacetime world cruise, Honolulu, proved to be his most memorable. The picture above is of Waikiki Beach, taken in 1940, and as it would have appeared to Frank when he visited the beach. He had turned fifteen on the day his toes nestled in its sands. After visiting Chinatown to buy jeans, and a trip to the YMCA, he and his friends swam in Waikiki's sheltered waters in front of the Royal Matson Hotel: with Diamond Point looming protectively over them in the backdrop. While lounging on these sun-kissed sands, Frank and his shipmates enjoyed their crew mess-room provided lunch bags. Each paper bagged meal comprised of the standard two sandwiches, one of cheese and the other of spam, with a small, not-so-fresh orange for 'afters'.

Frank and his friends lived a sweet life on that cruise, although it couldn't last. They were again sunbathing on a beach, this time in Havana, when on the 3rd September Frank heard that war had been declared.

Waikiki Beach in 1940 *Photo courtesy of Kamaaina56 Flickr Collection. © All rights reserved.*

The *Duchess of Richmond* immediately abandoned the remainder of her cruise programme and returned to Liverpool, where she resumed her regular pre-war runs to Montreal and Quebec. Her passenger lists were now mostly filled with the names of European evacuees escaping the onset of Nazism in their countries.

In the following photographs taken on board ship we can see Frank with some of the younger East European evacuees; on their way to Canada to build new lives and escape from Nazi tyranny.

Frank 'at work' on the *Duchess of Richmond*. Photo courtesy of the Frank Walker estate

AUTOMEDON:

With regard to his own future, I suspect only Frank knew what passed through his mind at this time.

The certificates of completed voyages recorded inside his discharge book show him to have decided to change not only his employer, but his department also.

He had paid off the *Duchess of Richmond* as a bellboy on the 21st August 1940 and joined Holt Lines' *'Automedon'* on 23rd September 1940, although as a deck boy, not as a catering boy as one might expect.

Frank obviously wanted a more secure future at sea than bell-hopping provided for him, and he sought to find it at sea in the deck department.

Blue Funnel Line, *S.S. Automedon* as a new ship. *Photo courtesy of the Frank Walker estate.*

How he managed to achieve this change is anybody's guess. Adolescents seeking employment at sea at this time had to undergo a stringent medical examination to prove themselves robust enough to deal safely with the tasks ahead of them. They also had to have attained a minimum height of 5'4"–and Frank had grown to only 4' 4" when he first went to sea, barely twelve months previously. How he managed to engineer himself past this obstacle remains another of those small mysteries that peppered his life. He had heard *Automedon* was about to sail and still had vacancies for crew that she hoped to fill prior to her departure. He applied on board and succeeded in securing a berth as a deck boy on 29th September 1940; the day before she sailed in convoy for Durban, and then independently to the Far East.

He had often remarked later that he had found life as a deck boy more arduous serving Holt's Blue Funnel Line cargo ships than had been the case when he worked as a bellboy on the Canadian Pacific passenger liners.

From his first day aboard *Automedon*, Frank claimed to have been constantly shouted at by a crewman nicknamed by his other shipmates as, 'The Terror of the China Sea.'

This man seemed set on making miserable the lives of the ship's junior ratings. However, being shouted at and teased was hardly a new experience for Frank. After all, he had grown up with a father and a cloister of nuns who had done little else but bawl at him throughout his earlier years. Nevertheless, Frank described his early days on *Automedon* as a happy time in his life.

Lloyds Register of Shipping lists her particulars as being launched in 1921, and described her as a refrigerated cargo-passenger ship of 7,528 Gross Register Tons and built for Ocean Steamships (Holt Line) by Palmers of Jarrow. A coal burner, nevertheless, a modern vessel of 459' in length overall, 58'4" in the beam, sailing on summer marks at 26'2". Twin steam turbines geared to a single shaft generating 6000 SHP propelled her at a designed laden service speed of 14.5 knots. On her bridge, *Automedon* boasted a single item of modern position finding equipment: a rather indifferently performing radio direction finder. She possessed no radar or any other electronic aids to navigation.

Her manifested cargo included: crated aircraft; motor vehicles and spare parts; whisky, cigarettes and foodstuffs that included seventy tons of frozen meats.

In her strong room she also carried 120 mailbags that concealed sensitive and classified documents, and six million Malay dollars in newly printed currency, all of which were bound for Singapore.

Automedon sailed for Freetown in convoy on 29th September, and thereafter sailed independently to Durban, where she arrived on the 25th October to load stores, provisions and bunkers prior to commencing her Far Eastern rotation.

Official records designated *Automedon* as a DEMS vessel – a Defensively Equipped Merchant Ship.

For self-defence, her armament consisted of an antiquated WW1, four-inch calibre gun similar to the piece fitted on *SS Maimoa* in the picture below.

Ordinarily, a trained DEMS gunner would be carried on board. A man who might be a retired artilleryman, or even one of the vessel's crew, if previously trained on a course ashore in the gun's management and firing procedures.

Gun crew training. SS Maimoa, 1939. *Photo courtesy of the Russ Dunshea89.wixsite.com website/dunshea-escapes1941*

Any engagement with an enemy warship would always have been a David and Goliath situation with scant chance of a successful outcome for *Automedon*. The gun's presence, however, did serve to instill a little confidence in the crew that they would be able to hit back should they

15

come abreast of a hostile vessel. In any event, most agreed that an old gun was better than having nothing whatsoever to hit back with. And, they believed they might just get lucky if such a scrap befell them.

* * *

Air Chief Marshal Sir Cyril Newall *Sir Cyril Newall, Governor General. Schmidt, Herman John, 1872-1959: Portrait and landscape negatives, Auckland district. Ref: 1/1-001914-F. Alexander Turnbull Library, Wellington, New Zealand. /records/22774654, Reproduced by kind permission of the Alexander Turnbull Library.*

Only her master knew that Air Chief Marshal Sir Cyril Newall, the Head of the Joint Chief of Staffs Committee, and a senior member of Churchill's War Cabinet had deposited in the captain's care on board *Automedon* a slender, weighted green bag with eyelets driven into its canvas to readily allow water ingress to ensure a rapid sinking should it become jettisoned on passage. The arrangement provided a robustly made and carefully prepared envelope in which to keep important documents secure, and carried a label that read:

'Top Secret – To be destroyed in the event of...'

The address on the package bore the name of the Commander in Chief of all British forces in the Far East: Sir Robert Brooke-Popham; together with a highest-level instruction that the envelope must be opened, and its content sighted, only by Sir Robert, and nobody else on the planet: such was the importance of its contents.

The package contained ultra-secret documents from the War Cabinet Planning Committee that included a full, unredacted copy of the Joint Chief of Staffs latest Far East Appreciation (August 1940). Its grim reading outlined the then current weaknesses of the British Empire's military strength in the region, and of Whitehall's inability (at that time) to apportion more forces to the area should they be needed if Japan entered the war on the side of Germany-as expected.

In the event that expectation should become real, the document contained full details of the operational availability of the resident RAF units, of the local naval strengths and an assessment of the roles of Australia and New Zealand.

Most piquant of all, a long paragraph contained up-to-date and copious notes on the fortifications of Singapore that listed their current condition and weaknesses. The package's contents provided a potential enemy with a full intelligence report prior to it embarking on a military adventure against the British possessions in the region.

Whatever had possessed Cyril Newall to place a precious intelligence asset at such perilous risk for its conveyance to Singapore on board a lumbering, slow, independently voyaging and virtually unarmed merchant vessel.

A more normal mode of transport would be to hold the valuable document fast and secure aboard a British warship. The answers to these questions remain a mystery.

Additionally, and perhaps even more serious to Newall's apparent blunder, is another unsolved unknown of why the *Automedon's* master, Captain William Brown Ewan did not jettison the document from the wing of the Bridge, in accordance with his instructions that were boldly written on the package, when the raider attacking him first hoisted her Nazi battle ensign. These questions continue to perplex historians.

There are papers written by learned observers who hold that superficial evidence exists to suggest this was not a mistake, but a grave ploy, a Churchill conspiracy to settle the doubt of whether or not Japan would enter the war allied to Germany by sacrificing Britain's Far East possessions to entice Japan into attacking the American fleet, thereby bringing the USA with its vast resources of material and manpower into the fight against Nazi tyranny. The opinions of these respected spectators paint a plausible current state of affairs with Churchill being faced with a Nazi invasion and having lost the bulk of his army at Dunkirk only weeks beforehand. In the course of time, history may resolve that open question.

The following is an account extracted from British and German records, and from individual statements of how *Automedon* came to arrive in her final position, and what eventually happened to her on 11th November 1940.

* * *

On sailing from Durban on the 29th October 1940, Capt. Ewan had shaped a course to pass south of Madagascar to his next port, Penang.

Second Officer, Donald Stewart had charge of the ship on the Bridge as officer of the watch for the morning watch. At about 0700 ship's time on the 11th November 1940 he sighted another vessel thirty-four degrees on the port bow, and on a course that would likely close with *Automedon*.

In fact, the vessels were steaming similar courses at this hour with *Automedon* actually overtaking, and closing with the other vessel.

Unable to identify the ship's form when she had first appeared above the horizon, Stewart called the master in compliance with Captain Ewan's Bridge standing orders.

Captain Ewan then joined his second officer on the bridge, and in silent togetherness they observed the approach of the other vessel. According to Kapitan Rogge's memoir, he had now turned his ship and had altered its course towards *Automedon* without yet revealing its true identity as *Atlantis*.

Ewan and Stewart observed the other vessel for several minutes after which Captain Ewan remarked to Stewart of his belief that the vessel was of a Dutch configuration. He thus determined it safe to continue on the present course, since the latest Royal Navy reports he had received on board had advised of the presence of hostile raiders and U-boats operating to the north of Madagascar, and *Automedon* had passed clear of their threat to the south of the island.

Nevertheless, Stewart asked if he should adjust the course to starboard in order to pass well clear of the other vessel that now appeared to be on a converging course with *Automedon*. His question received no answer from Captain Ewan, and so he maintained their present course without making any adjustments to the ship's planned track.

At about 0730, helmsman Stanley Hugill overheard the master say to Stewart that he still thought the other vessel to be a Dutch ship, and that he believed they had come far enough east for them to be out of danger of attack by enemy raiders and U-boats.

The *Automedon's* radio room had picked up a distress call from two other ships in this area on the previous day, each one ostensibly reporting attacks. They included one from *Ole Jacob* a Norwegian tanker from a position quite close to them. After due consideration of the message's irregular format, Captain Ewan had considered the transmission to have been a false alarm, and he ignored the communication.

It transpires that the Norwegian's call had been manipulated and interfered with by the German surface raider, *Atlantis*, who had subsequently attacked and captured the *Ole Jacob:* taking her intact along with her cargo of 10,000 tons of precious aviation spirit.

According to a later report by 2/O Stewart, Captain Ewan's mind at this time had been fully occupied with his concern for reaching the later planned course alteration eastwards to steam directly towards Penang, their next port of call. He had previously set a course to pass safely through the strong and complex currents of the Bengal Strait north of Sumatra, and then on into the northern Malacca Strait and thence to Georgetown Harbour on Penang's eastern coast.

Captain Ewan had planned to make this change at night, without benefit of radar or shore lights, relying only on the ship's celestial navigation, dead reckoning and a rather contrary and rarely trustworthy radio direction finder to make a safe passage. Indian Ocean weather in November is often very agreeable, with warm temperatures and clear blue skies for most of the month.

With regards to the present convergence, Captain Ewan had decided to maintain his present course and speed and then left the Bridge to return to his cabin.

Second Officer Stewart entered in the logbook, 'course to be maintained'; and he conveyed the Master's order to his relief, Third Officer Peter Whitaker, at eight bells (0800).

* * *

Captain Ewan, has been described as a dour man of medium build, in his early fifties, yet sporting a full head of silvery hair. The officers and crew found him to be of a rather taciturn nature. He enjoyed the respect of his crew, who found Captain William Ewan of Hartlepool to be a strict disciplinarian and a master who nevertheless exuded dignity and confidence, while for most of the time on board he surrounded himself with an unapproachable attitude.

Yet for such an experienced and confident shipmaster, Captain Ewan appears to have made a number of serious errors of judgement on that Armistice Day in 1940.

For example, had he followed Stewart's suggestion and *Automedon* had turned her bow more to starboard and steamed away at 14 knots–a speed well within her laden and mechanical capacity–she might have eluded her pursuer. Such an alteration would have taken her closer to the friendly-navy patrolled shipping lanes operating along the Sumatran coastline.

Kapitan Rogge of *Atlantis* would then have likely shied away to avoid the possibility of contact with hostile naval forces. That, of course, is unsupported supposition. It fits, however, with the nature and practice of Rogge in previous and later engagements.

The commander of the Atlantis, Kapitan s.z., Bernhard Rogge, did mention something to that effect to Donald Stewart on an occasion when they chatted together onboard *Atlantis* a day or two following the attack on *Automedon*.

Fourth Engineer, Sam Harper had overheard this conversation and repeated its content when interviewed by the American Consul in Marseilles following his successful escape from France in early 1941.

THE ATTACK:

In an interview in 1962, Second Officer Stewart stated that on being relieved at 0800, he went down directly to his cabin. At around 0820, while he stood shaving in his underwear, he heard the sound of gunfire. He looked out of his porthole, sited adjacent to the Master's accommodation, and was astonished to see the presumed Dutch ship now flying Swastika colours and steaming in much closer proximity to, and on a parallel course with *Automedon*.

He rushed from his cabin to rouse Extra Second Officer Wilson and then woke First Officer Peter Evan. Stewart then followed them both in a mad scramble to the Bridge. On his way there, Stewart noticed the two Radio Officers still busily transmitting the 'RRR- I am being attacked' distress signal, without realising that *Atlantis'* radio technicians were jamming their output.

Stewart said, there followed a thunderous bang, the blast of which tossed his body into the air like it was nothing more than a leaf, and landed him unconscious on the bridge deck.

Helmsman Stanley Hugill had not been relieved on the wheel at the time of this explosion. He became almost buried in the debris that followed the blast, but luckily he had escaped from more serious harm.

Stewart had run out of his cabin undressed, and with shaving soap covering his chin. Fate decreed that he should survive, whereas the Captain and five others that included Wilson and Whittaker, his recent relief, had perished in the detonation that had also destroyed the Wheelhouse and Chartroom.

Ewan's decision not to adjust *Automedon's* course had thus sealed her fate.

Within an hour of first being wakened by Stewart, Captain Ewan now lay dead with three brother officers among the chaos and debris that had been his Bridge: while twelve crewmen lay wounded, and three other crewmembers lay dead in other spaces around the ship.

* * *

From Atlantis's war diary, and repeated in Kapitan Rogge's memoirs, we learn that the ships detected the presence of each other at about the same time.

In the morning watch on the Atlantis, Able Seaman Jena stood lookout duty in the raider's foremast crow's nest and reported a smudge of smoke on the horizon.

Rogge ordered his crew to action stations and steered a course to intercept the vessel, believing it to be *Automedon*.

It appears from this memoir that he might have been informed of her heading his way, but that is supposition based upon captured Italian secret service papers found in Berlin at the end of the war.

At 0758 her war diary placed the ships 4,600 metres apart (two and a half miles).

At 0803 Atlantis revealed her true identity by hoisting her Swastika battle ensign together with the International Code of Signal flags for:

'Do Not Raise Alarm' and another ordering *Automedon* to 'STOP'.'

Minutes later the vessels stood just over three cables apart (600 metres) and Atlantis augmented her signals by firing a double warning shot from her forward gun across *Automedon's* bow.

The awful tragedy that subsequently befell *Automedon* was about to unfold.

* * *

It was too late by the time *Atlantis* showed her true colours, and impossible anyway, for Captain Ewan–had he lived–to extricate himself from this close quarters situation and prevent the ensuing assault by *Atlantis*.

Before the Bridge exploded, and according to a later report made by helmsman Stan Hugill, the Bridge team were staggered by the suddenness of the confrontation, and found they were unable to decode the signal flags fast enough for the German raider's satisfaction.

Meanwhile in the Radio Shack, 1st Radio Officer John Rawcliffe and 2nd Radio Officer Philip Buck continued to carry out the captain's order to transmit an RRR message, and to do so repetitively until he told them to stop.

Unknown to them, and as they continued to key the distress message, *Atlantis* had commenced jamming their transmission only two seconds after the initial broadcast. In consequence, only the latitude of the encounter escaped onto the airwaves of the listening world.

Hugill recalled that he heard Captain Ewan order the wheel put hard a starboard and so put *Automedon's* stern to the raider to present the smallest target to *Atlantis*. Hugill said in an interview that he had repeated and executed the master's command, and then heard the captain shout out vigorously,

'Come on everybody. Let's do it! We're going to fight.'

A Balaclava moment indeed!

* * *

And where was Frank Walker while this tragic drama played out on the Bridge?

Just before eight bells, Frank stood with Bill Diggle, the ship's carpenter, at the after end of the port side amidships centre castle. Together they watched *Atlantis* approach them in open-mouthed astonishment. This mysterious vessel now appeared to be heading directly towards them.

Bill ran off to collect his binoculars, and when he came back, he and Frank took turns with the glasses to observe the ensuing developments.

By Frank's reckoning, the time stood at about 0830 when the fireworks began, and he recalled the sea being as flat as plate glass. Later, he thought it funny the things one remembers at highly emotive times.

Before she had revealed herself under the Swastika flag, Bill Diggle had reckoned *Atlantis* to be a friendly intermediate cargo and passenger vessel belonging to the 'P and O' company. He and Frank continued to watch in growing alarm as the distance between the ships continued to close, with neither vessel appearing to make any attempt to adjust course to avoid an impending collision.

Frank next recalled seeing sparks flying from Atlantis's starboard side, followed by four puffs of white smoke. By this time, she lay just forward of *Automedon's* port beam. Frank then recollected hearing a loud bang followed by an almighty crash above and around him.

This would have been the first, in-earnest, salvo of shot fired from *Atlantis* that followed on from her prior warning shots across *Automedon's* bows. These next shells exploded on the bridge deck, directly above where Bill and Frank were standing.

More salvoes followed in swift succession–all of which landed on the centre castle housing where the Navigating Bridge, officers' accommodation and saloon were located. Frank recollects that following each strike, *Automedon* gave him the impression of the ship shuddering, and screaming its protest.

Assistant Steward Alan Parsons stood a few aft of Frank and Bill Diggle. He ran in panic to the starboard side as the first shells exploded on board. Unluckily for him, shrapnel from the second salvo caught him as he passed by Number Three Hatch. The hatch coaming had fully protected his lower body from the blast. Unfortunately, his upper body had remained exposed, and this is where he sustained severe injuries. In acute pain, he managed to stagger towards a deck lavatory, where he collapsed on the deck outside and lost consciousness.

A German boarding party stumbled upon him later and swiftly zipped him into a body bag and whisked him off to their hospital for surgery aboard Atlantis.

Parsons had recovered consciousness by this time and remembers having to wait his turn while the two German surgeons worked on Chief Steward Percy Mosely, who lived at Heswall on the Wirral. It had been Frank who had found and first tended to the wounded Chief Steward.

The surgeons eventually did an excellent job on Parsons, who recovered fully. However, he had to carry remnants of shrapnel buried deep inside his chest for the remainder of his life.

The blast had come as a shock for Frank. Though stunned, he remembered holding his body rigid, and tensed himself to remain standing firm as the blast passed him by.

The awning above his head became shredded, while the stanchions that hadn't been blown away had become twisted and buckled. Frank believed it a marvel that he had remained uninjured.

He turned to talk to carpenter Bill Diggle, only to find the man nowhere to be seen. For reasons known only to himself, the carpenter had bolted forward.

Frank's attention next settled on the solo attempt of one of the crewmembers to lower a Carley liferaft into the water from the poop deck.

Then another seaman, possibly the ship's gunner, caught Frank's eye as the man ran towards *Automedon's* four-inch gun mounted on the after deck.

Frank observed the raider had moved and now stood off close on *Automedon's* port quarter.

He said, 'she was now so near I could see and hear an officer on her bridge shouting to us through a loudhailer, in English':

'Don't go near the gun or we'll blow you out of the water.'

Frank's ears were ringing, but on the rare occasions he spoke of the incident in later life, he always claimed that he heard this warning quite clearly.

Atlantis' 5.9" Main Armament rigged for action. *Photo © Courtesy of www.wrecksite.eu*

This episode is also recorded in the *Atlantis's* war diary, and translates as follows:

'Bombardment resumed, although transmissions had ceased because a figure was seen approaching the gun on the after deck of *Automedon*– which had turned its stern toward Atlantis.'

The Germans thought the Blue Funnel liner was about to fight back, and Rogge had ordered three more salvoes to be fired on to the fo'c'sle and poop decks as a deterrent.

In justification for the resumption of the bombardment, Captain Rogge wrote in his memoir: 'I deduced from the man apparently running for the gun after the vessel had apparently turned its stern to *Atlantis* that *Automedon* was about to fight back. With repairs difficult to engineer for a ship such as this, raiders' crews took even the slightest risk seriously.'

This episode left Frank with a sour taste in his mouth for the rest of his life. He recalled with the utmost disdain the total absence of any machine gun or rifle fire coming from *Atlantis* to counter the threat of the single, running man.

Frank said, 'the ships were so close by each other that a single rifle shot would have downed the man running for the gun, but Rogge decided instead to use his artillery–and at such close range. Why didn't he shoot the man instead of landing a further barrage on an already crippled ship and kill and maim more of her crew?'

On those uncommon occasions when Frank could be goaded to talk about this particular incident, he invariably finished the account by saying,

'Barely a day goes by since then that I don't ask myself that question.'

Atlantis' war diary further records: 'twelve shells were fired at *Automedon* in rapid succession, and at point blank range. All were on target.'

* * *

Frank ran inside the now wrecked deck below the bridge housing. This is where he came across Chief Steward, Percy Mosely lying on the deck, and in a bad way. He said, 'I could see he had lost a lot of blood. He was cold and writhing in agony.' Frank found a blanket in a nearby cabin and covered him up as best he could, then gave him a drink of water. He said, 'I didn't know what else I could do for him. Then he grabbed my arm and asked me to find an envelope in his cabin and pass it on to the 2nd Steward–which later on, I did.

It turned out to be a ready-made 'good bye' letter to Percy Mosely's family. The Chief Steward had previously written in readiness should he be unfortunate enough to suffer the calamity that had now befallen him.

Frank said, 'I guess he knew he was dying. It was hard for me to console the man. I could see his life was ebbing away. I then noticed Assistant Steward Alex Parsons from Wallasey lying on the deck on the other side of the hatchway. He had his chest all smashed up. It was eerie because it was quiet after all the shellfire noise. It was like a deathly silence had fallen over the ship.

'The next thing I knew the Germans had arrived carrying revolvers and with hand grenades fixed on their belts. I could see they were well armed and by their determined manner ready for any situation. I don't think they were proud of their handiwork. They became very subdued when they witnessed the carnage and devastation they had caused us with their 5.9"shells.

'We were sitting ducks to them. The boarding party were thorough going about their business. It was like they knew exactly where to go, what to do and when and how to do what it was they had to do. I found out later they'd had plenty of practice. We were their thirteenth victim in just over six months.'

Interestingly, a page in Rogge's personal diary records: '*Automedon's* master had ignored my warnings–and he paid for it with his life.' Rogge justified his action by adding 'my own survival depended on no alarms being raised.'

* * *

Frank continues with the story. 'The boarding party set about looking after the ship's injured and dying. The badly wounded were rapidly sent across to the *Atlantis* where they received proper medical and surgical treatment in the mini-hospital they had on board. Sad, but Chief

Steward Moseley and AB Joe Watts, from Albert Edward Road, Liverpool, both died shortly after being transferred to the raider.

Shell damage to Automedon's Fo'c'sle *Photo courtesy of the estate of Frank Walker*

'Even the fo'c'sle head had been hit with their shells. The forward portside rails had been ripped from their mountings and lay around the deck in macabre twisted sculptures.

'They found the chippie lying dead beside the windlass. Bill Diggle from London wouldn't have known what hit him when that shell landed beside him.

'Why he had bolted forward when the shelling started is anybody's guess?

'All the boats and their davits were smashed and fragmented. The funnel had some gaping holes in quite a few places. The bridge and the officer's deck below it was completely destroyed and in a shambles.

'In a matter of five minutes we had four dead, with two dying and a dozen more wounded–some of them were seriously hurt.

'We also had fifty-six Chinese seamen as part of our crew. They were on their way back to Hong Kong. One of them received a right serious wound below the belt and lamented his loss, gripping his crotch and shrieking in agonised *pidgin* English. It would have been funny had it not been for real. I never did find out if the poor blighter made it through at all.'

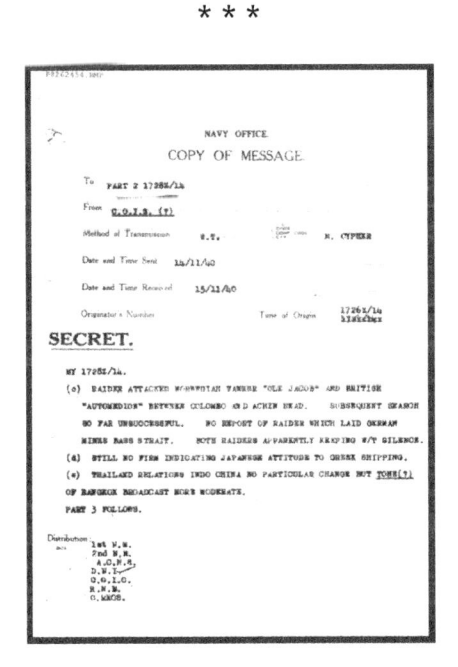

* * *

Loss of Automedon: Part 2 of a Royal Australian Navy secret message 1940 *From the archives of Frank W Walker, courtesy of Mrs. Vera Walker*

One would have thought the loss of *Automedon*, and with it the possibility of the enemy capturing the ultra-secret document she carried would have motivated every person, plane and powers-that-be to seek her out and find the truth and extent of the disaster that had transpired.

But the British military and government decision makers decided instead to ignore her loss, and to act as if it had never happened: maintaining this false pretence until long after the war had ended. The Australian navy sent out a sole secret message three days later that mentioned *Automedon*, although there appears to have been no actual naval follow up to clarify any of the uncertainties it raised. It seemed as if

29

the authorities believed that the *Automedon* had managed to lose herself at sea.

* * *

Another intriguing mystery concerns the requirement under the Merchant Shipping Acts of those days concerning a ships owners' legal requirements following the loss of one of their ships without trace when at sea. They were obliged under a lawfully imposed time limit of one month to deliver a copy of the missing Crew Articles of Agreement to a Mercantile Marine Office Superintendent. This would be a copy of the collective contract document binding seafarers to a ship, and vice versa, until completion of the voyage and the agreement. This process would have legally closed their contracts on their behalf, and stating the reasons for any loss of life and the ship.

Mr. Shipston of Holt Line prepared the replacement copy for the *Automedon* and then submitted it for closure to the Mercantile Marine Office in Birkenhead on 14th January 1941. I hold a copy of the Articles he submitted on that day. And they are meticulously made up.

It accurately lists those who had lost their lives and those who had become prisoners of war. Now therein lies another peculiar mystery. How on earth could Mr. Shipston have known before the 14th January 1941, which of those men had died on board *Automedon* and which men had been captured and made into prisoners of war only two months after the attack?

The *Automedon* crew hadn't yet reached a shore and were still being held as captives aboard a German supply ship on that particular day in January 1941.

The Red Cross could not possibly have been involved so soon after the attack. Of one thing that does seem certain, irrespective of Kapitan Rogge being a humane gentleman of the sea, he would not have cabled the British Department of Transport in London and supplied them with these particulars.

With Whitehall apparently doing its utmost subsequent to the attack to deny to the world the loss of *Automedon* to a raider, how could this information have been officially obtained? How could it even be possible for Mr. Shipston of Holt's to have known these details in order to accurately complete these documents and present them on time? But he did, and that mystery, if such it is remains to be explained away.

* * *

Sixteen-year-old Frank Walker now found himself to be a POW aboard the vessel that had attacked plundered and then scuttled his ship.

But Frank wasn't the youngest captive taken into confinement aboard *Atlantis* during the month of November 1940. That dubious honour belongs to fifteen-year-old Leslie McDermott-Brown, an apprentice taken from Paddy Henderson's, *S.S. Kemmandine*–an *Atlantis* victim on another day.

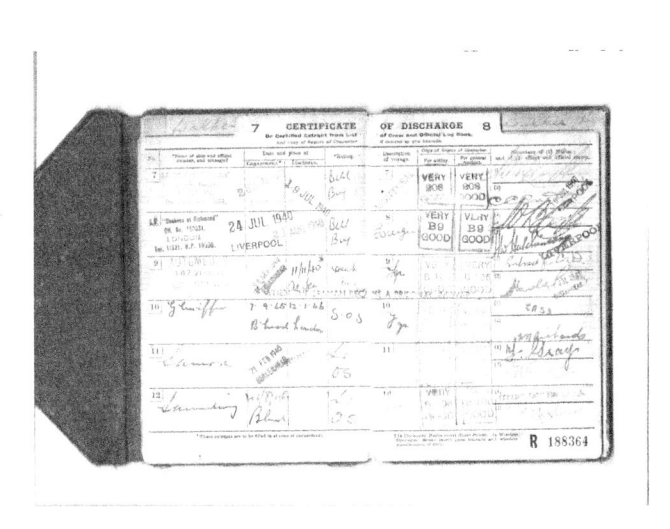

Frank Walker's Merchant Navy Discharge Book
Reproduced by kind permission of Mrs Vera Walker.

In the picture above one can see Frank's Discharge book now properly made up for the day he went into captivity as a prisoner of war from the *Automedon;* with him going off articles, and also off pay on 11th November 1940.

In those days and for many years after the war, whenever ships were lost at sea their voyages were deemed completed and the seamen released from the ship's articles. It meant they went off pay on that day, notwithstanding they might still be at sea and battling an ocean's waves for their survival in a flimsy lifeboat, with their families hiding from the rent man when he called for lack of money to pay him.

And there's another small mystery arising here that one might wish to ponder?

This extract is from Frank's original discharge book. The one issued to him when he first entered the Merchant Navy from school in 1939. It lists all of his earlier Canadian Pacific voyages and contains these certificates of service, which are complete and intact inside the book. The document is not a copy.

The mystery is this. How on earth did the book survive the attack on *Automedon* and Frank's incarceration in Germany for five years for him to have it ready to use again once he continued his seafaring career following his release from captivity? How did Frank even get hold of it, before or after leaving the *Automedon* before the Germans sank her in the Indian Ocean?

The author will offer his thoughts on this topic later in this account.

ATLANTIS:

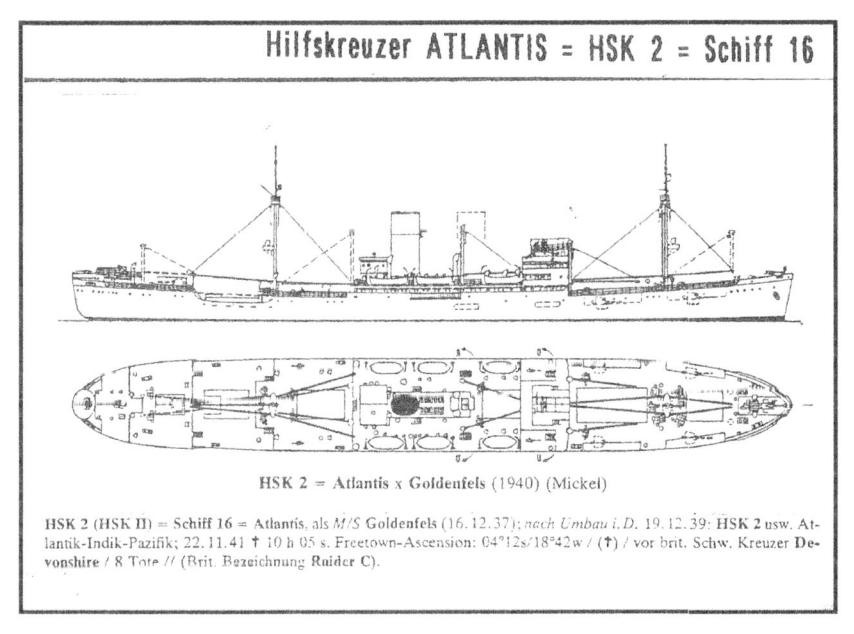

Hilfskreuzer ATLANTIS = HSK 2 = Schiff 16

HSK 2 = Atlantis x Goldenfels (1940) (Mickel)

HSK 2 (HSK II) = Schiff 16 = Atlantis, als M/S Goldenfels (16.12.37); nach Umbau i.D. 19.12.39: HSK 2 usw. Atlantik-Indik-Pazifik; 22.11.41 † 10 h 05 s. Freetown-Ascension: 04°12s/18°42w / (†) / vor brit. Schw. Kreuzer Devonshire / 8 Tote // (Brit. Bezeichnung Raider C).

Diagram of Atlantis, showing arrangement for rigging a dummy funnel
© *Courtesy of www.wrecksite.eu.*

How did she and her ilk come into being?

Gross Admiral Erich Raeder ran Hitler's navy for the years before the war. He built a new force of sleek capital ships, albeit tiny in numbers when compared to the massive strength of the Royal Navy that it would have to face in battle whenever war came. Britain and its Empire, he reckoned, would be Germany's greatest adversary if and when war ensued. He knew Britain required fifty-five million tons of imports to sustain it through 1939, and would require increasing volumes of imports in subsequent years, especially if it had to face Germany at war. The prime task of his navy, therefore, would be to interfere with the flow of Britain's commerce. His new surface warships, with their large crews, would be insufficient and likely to be hunted down at sea by the Royal Navy's vastly superior fleet numbers. Germany had hitherto been denied submarines under the Versailles Treaty that had ended WW1, and Raeder's mind settled on armed merchant cruisers–warships disguised as merchant vessels, and a development of the successful 'Q' ship concept of WW1.

In 1937 he ordered seven cargo ships to be built for commercial operation in the DDG-Hansa merchant shipping company. He ordered some modifications built into their construction to enable their rapid conversion into surface raiders whenever the Kriegsmarine (Hitler's navy) might have a need of such vessels to serve the Third Reich as warships.

Atlantis, known also as *Schiff-16*, proved to be the most successful of these half-cruisers. Constructed as a 5-hatch vessel of 7,862 GRT 155m LOA (Length Over All), 18.7m beam powered by 2 x 6 cylinder diesel engines on a single shaft and she sailed on a summer draft of 8.7m (29').

Commissioned as an armed cruiser on the 19th December 1939, when her rapidly mounted armament consisted of:

6 x 15cm (5.9") naval guns	1 x 75 mm (3") gun
2 x twin 37mm (1.5") A/A guns	2 x twin 2 cm (.79") cannons
4 x 533mm torpedo tubes and	93 x maritime contact mines.

She also carried 2 x Heinkel seaplanes, and was equipped with a dummy funnel and variable height masts to facilitate her disguise into emulating the configuration of other nation's merchant ships.

Her complement comprised 367 officers and men. To maintain her merchant vessel subterfuge, she concealed her weaponry behind pivoting false deck structures.

To maintain her pretence when stalking, or sailing in close quarters with other vessels Rogge would have his crewmen parade about her decks dressed as nannies while wheeling baby-carriages and perambulators to enhance the warship's disguise as an intermediate merchant ship with passengers on board.

Her singular function was to patrol the vastnesses of the South Atlantic and Indian Oceans to attack British and allied tonnage. She received fuel and essential supplies when required by replenishments at sea, through the German network of purpose built supply ships such as *Thor* and *Altmark*.

Atlantis at sea, disguised as a merchant vessel. *Photo © Courtesy of www.wrecksite.eu*

Photos Courtesy of www.wrecksite.eu

35

The above is a photo *of Atlantis* sporting a favourite disguise as the *SS Antenor*, another Ocean Steamships (Holt) liner, later commandeered by the Royal Navy and employed as the Armed Merchant Cruiser *HMS Antenor*.

U-128 took this picture of *Atlantis* while on patrol in the South Atlantic.

Poster © Courtesy of www.wrecksite.eu

Kapitan zur See Bernhard Rogge. *Photo ©
www.wrecksite.eu*

Raeder had chosen well when he selected Kapitan zur see Bernhard Rogge as *Atlantis'* commander.

Rogge had long proven himself as a highly professional sailor who eventually saw service in four German navies. He first served in the Kaiser's navy and saw action at Jutland on the battle cruiser *SMS 'Moltke'*. During the Weimar Republic he commanded the then German navy's sail training ship, *'S.V. Albert Leo Schlagter'*.

When Hitler's navy arrived, enormous problems arose to hinder him, since he had a Jewish grandmother and under the prevailing law that made him into a Jew also. As such, he could not legally occupy any government office or take up any official appointment whatsoever. This state of affairs proved to be a major problem for Raeder, who badly wanted Rogge for his commander of the *Atlantis*.

In a final attempt to execute a solution, Raeder approached Hitler directly on Rogge's behalf and managed to persuade the Fuhrer to grant him a *Mishinge*. A German Blood Declaration that allowed Rogge to describe himself as Aryan in official government documents.

Being now officially of German blood, Rogge could take up his planned appointment and Raeder obtained his commander of choice. Rogge justified Raeder's faith in him by becoming the most successful of all of his surface raiders, having sunk twenty-two ships totalling 145,960 GRT during the 655 consecutive days of his time at sea in command of *Atlantis*.

There remained, however, a sting in the tail for Rogge. The blood document issued to him by Dr. Walter Gross's Ministry for Racial Affairs added a caustic condition in the final line at the bottom of this lengthy page that otherwise declared his acceptable racial situation. The line in tiny print declared that the award of his Aryan acceptance would be subject to review on the cessation of hostilities. Rogge had, in fact, received an 'Hostilities Only' relief from the Third Reich's pernicious race laws.

Although the SA (*Sturmabteilung*)–the para-military wing of the official Nazi party–no longer tormented or attacked Rogge, as it had done with impunity beforehand. This relief, unfortunately, did not extend to his family. His wife and her mother were also born with a Jewish grandmother and mother respectively, and as such also became registered at law as Jewish. The vigour of the hounding and torment directed at these ladies by the SA became so intolerable that they were both grievously driven to commit suicide in April 1939.

On the day that Bernhard Rogge took command of Atlantis, after having interred his wife and her mother, he found that he had only his career and a small terrier (Ferry) left to him.

Rogge, the son of a Lutheran minister, had grown up as an enigmatic and devoutly religious man. He became a humane seaman, who readily earned the respect of his men, and of his captives, whom he would walk among with his little dog to talk to them individually.

Yet, ironically, although he performed the securing of victory for Hitler's regime to his utmost ability–as indeed his duty bound him to deliver. On a personal level, however, a total victory for Hitler would become a pyrrhic victory for himself–since it would immediately result in him being re-assessed for Jewish bloodlines. The day Germany might win the war would likely be the day that The Reich he had served so well might discard him from its national midst as just another unwanted Jew. One wonders about his thoughts on this prospect, for he appeared to harbour no fanatical zeal or even liking for Nazism.

Once the West German navy became established at the end of the war, Rogge served as a *Vizeadmiral* in the post-war Nato forces: the fourth navy in which he saw service.

Burial at sea, *Photo courtesy of the Frank Walker Estate.*

In 1940, meanwhile, Rogge conducted himself and commanded his ship in the nobler traditions of the sea. He had lost an able seaman to sunstroke in the Indian Ocean. The above is a picture of that rating's burial at sea. The ship's company were assembled in their best uniforms to afford full military honours to the deceased.

* * *

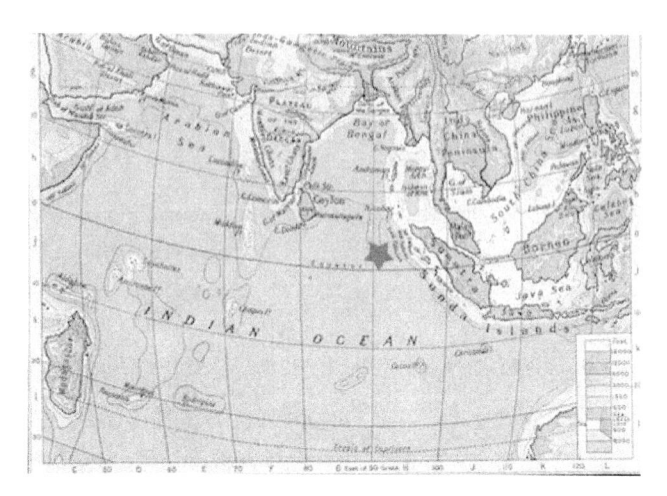

Approximate site of the attack, November 11th 1940
Reproduced by Courtesy from Bartholomew's Graphic Atlas 10th Edition 1956

The star on the above chart shows the approximate location where *Atlantis* attacked the *Automedon*. It took place in a position approximately 250 miles WSW of Banda Aceh, at the entrance to the Bengal Strait for onward passage to her next port of call, Penang–on the northern, west coast of Malaya.

This location lies away from the main shipping lanes of that time. Captain Rogge hastened the transfer of plunder from *Automedon* in the event another vessel might happen along, see the two stationary vessels close by each other and realise what was happening. Rogge wished to avoid the possibility of discovery, and of a radio message being sent to the British and Australian warships that were actively hunting these German raiders in the Indian Ocean. Rogge set a time limit of three hours for his piracy operation, and persuaded the ship's crew to assist in the transfer of stores and other material from *Automedon* to *Atlantis*. It is said they did this willingly to avoid waste and in gratitude for being allowed fifteen minutes to collect their own personal possessions prior to their transfer to *Atlantis* and captivity.

* * *

According to international maritime law, Rogge and his crew had committed an act of piracy by attacking and robbing *Automedon* on the high seas. This, however, is not the place to discuss points of pertinent international law.

Was Rogge actually expecting *Automedon* to appear over his horizon?

A good question, and a query raised by several eminent academics after the event. Rogge does not specifically say so in his memoirs or in the *Atlantis's* war diary, however, powerful evidence exists to suggest the *Atlantis* might have been searching for *Automedon*.

When she had called at Durban, *Automedon* appears to have become a marked ship by an Italian secret service cell operating inside the port. They then passed on her details to the Abwehr–the German secret service with whom they worked in close co-ordination as allies in 1940.

Papers found in Berlin at the end of the war support this premise. Yet a rumour cannot be verified that an Italian submarine tracked her when she resumed her passage to Penang subsequent to her departure from Durban.

Many of Rogge's attacks were executed by subterfuge and trickery, and they often succeeded without a shot being fired. In those cases the whole ship would be captured, including her codebooks–as happened following the attack on *S.S. Port Wellington*. The Germans could, therefore, monitor *Automedon's* coded position messages without any difficulty.

When *Atlantis'* lookout, AB Jena, spotted smoke on the horizon, and Rogge had checked it out, he wrote in his memoir:

'We spotted each other at about the same time. As she came more into view I could recognise the graceful Blue Funnel lines of *Automedon*.'

Which faintly suggests he might have been expecting to see her appear?

* * *

The attack on *Automedon* proceeded as described earlier in this account. Boarding parties went aboard her under the command of Rogge's First Lieutenant, Ulrich Mohr.

The extent of the destruction they had caused surprised even the German boarding party. Another entry in the *Atlantis'* war diary records:

'The *Automedon* presented itself as a picture of devastation.'

In a television interview after the war, Leutnant zur see Ulrich Mohr, the leader of the German boarding party said, 'the close range shelling had destroyed virtually every structure above the hull and there was nothing left undamaged.'

He wrote of it in his own memoir: 'I was horrified to see the death, bloodshed and the mangled remains of the ship's superstructures caused by just a few shells.'

He wrote also of an eerie silence that prevailed over the shocking extent of the devastation. Silence, save for the sound of escaping steam from broken pipes: much the same eeriness that Frank had mentioned earlier.

* * *

We now pick up the tale in Frank's words once again:

'The German boarding parties set about ransacking the ship. They used us to help transfer stores and goods. They took all of the frozen meat, all the fags and other stores plus 550 cases of Scotch whisky. Transporting it all in a small fleet of motorboats across to the Atlantis.

'While some of them opened the hatches, others set about breaking into the strong room, making a systematic search like they were looking for something in particular. It astonished us when we found out later, all of what they did find.

'We didn't know we were carrying highly confidential documents in with the mail. Out of the 120 bags of mail for the troops in Singapore, we heard they got fifteen bags of navy cypher tables, Royal Navy sailing orders, government papers, new Merchant Navy codes, and loads of other secret documents.

'But even that prize haul was nothing compared to the document they found when they decided to go rummaging around in the ruins and debris that had been the ship's Bridge and Chart Room.

'There they found an envelope from the Planning Department of the War Cabinet in Whitehall addressed to the C. in. C. British Far East Forces, no less: and for his eyes alone. We found out later that it gave a highly detailed evaluation of the British military strength in the region with details of its lack of naval power along with instructions to the RAF for the defence of Singapore. It even listed their available aircraft types and the airworthy numbers of each kind of 'plane. It said in writing that 'Japan must know Britain would be unable to send more aircraft', and that the 'British Far East Fleet was seriously under strength'.

It remarked on Japan's desire for expansion, and the report concluded that Britain must avoid aggravating Japan even if this meant making economic concessions to them, something that both Britain and the USA had always opposed, until then.

'This top-secret document included detailed notes on the present defences of Singapore and an assessment of the role Australia and New Zealand should play in the event of Japan entering the war. It had everything a potential foe with his eyes on Singapore and beyond would wish for–and even more yet.

'Like all the other things from the strong room, this was marked:

"Classified–destroy in an emergency."

'It is highly likely that Capt Ewan did not know of the secret documents hidden in the mailbags in his strong-room, and he could not have got them out for disposal even if he had wished to do so, but he certainly would have known about the Far East Appreciation report found in the destroyed chartroom–because he alone had it put in his personal charge.

'It is a reasonable assumption that he had been briefed of the necessity to dispose of it over the side should there be a risk of it ever becoming exposed to an enemy. It said so on the canvas envelope, after all, and he kept it in the chartroom, ready at hand to heave it over the side from the bridge wing in the event of any serious trouble. But he didn't, and the Germans got hold of it, and they passed a copy across to the Japs.'

* * *

Whether or not Captain Ewan had sufficient time before he died in the shelling to dispose of this intelligence is an exoneration that history will likely deny him. Whatever the circumstances of his personal situation, this precious document now resided in German hands.

Rogge and Mohr both had a command of English and, as their first reports state that they pored over this intelligence cornucopia with unbelieving eyes. Rogge eventually considered the document to be a true find. In his memoir he notes being troubled at first about its authenticity because he had found it on an elderly and virtually unarmed merchantman. Because of the letter's strategic importance he would have expected it of being more securely conveyed on a warship.

He sent them all without delay to Admiral Wenneker, the ex-commander of the heavy cruiser *Deutschland*, and the then German naval attaché in Tokyo. Rogge sent him this find aboard the *Ole Jacob*, the Norwegian prize tanker he had previously captured, for further on sending to Berlin for their consideration. Berlin decided the material should be shared with the Japanese government as an encouragement for them to join the war allied to Germany.

Thus, this ultra secret document passed into enemy hands and actively served to accelerate Japan's entry into the war, with the devastating effect of extending what until then had been an essentially European fight into a worldwide conflict.

Admiral Yamamoto, the architect of Pearl Harbour, claimed to maintain a quiet confidence that in the event of a clash, his aircraft carriers could wipe out the US Pacific Fleet, but he harboured the compelling fear of a certainty that he would have to face a British fleet in retaliation should he do so. And he believed Japan did not possess sufficient resources to split its Grand Fleet and to engage two opposing fleets in battle and succeed.

The *Automedon* papers removed that fear from him, and helped propel the Japanese Empire into war with the United States just a year later, and ultimately into its own nuclear destruction.

* * *

Before we leave the *Automedon* to her fate, we have to mention Mrs. Ferguson's tea-set, if only for completeness. This is a story that resounds through British archives in great detail, but is unsubstantiated in their German counterparts.

The following is largely supposition on the author's part. A belief, nevertheless, that is supported by the similar opinions of a number of more learned and august academic authorities than himself.

The promulgated British story has all of the hallmarks of the chinless wonder fiction writers employed at this time in Broadway Buildings, the former London premises occupied by the present day residents of Thames House (MI6). Their job at that time being solely to write plausible untruths in order to conceal sensitive facts, or to aid ministerial desired deceptions or manipulations. What makes their lies plausible is the peppering of true facts throughout their stories.

It is a fact that Violet Ferguson and her Irish husband, Alan Ferguson, were embarked as passengers on *Automedon* when she was attacked, and then were imprisoned aboard *Atlantis*. They were returning to Singapore where he worked as a ship's engineer with Straits Steamships– a subsidiary company of Holt Line.

A rather over-elaborate story beloved of historical fiction bloggers exists to blame Violet Ferguson for the Germans entering the *Automedon's* strong room and thereby finding the Codes and sensitive materials secured in the mailbags that they discovered therein.

The story runs that boarding officer Ulrich Mohr; being pressed for time by Rogge to complete the plundering of the ship, had not located the strong room secreted in the fo'c'sle. Mohr had looked at his watch, called time on the transfer of stores and given *Automedon's* crew fifteen minutes to pack a small case of personal belongings before transferring them to Atlantis. That last part is proven to be factually correct.

Mrs. Ferguson is then reputed to have approached Mohr and asked if he would get her prized tea-set out of the 'not wanted on voyage' baggage room that happened also to be the strong room located in the fo'c'sle. Mohr is said to have obliged the lady, opened the strong room and therein found an intelligence treasure trove.

In his memoir, Mohr does not recall this conversation and he talks more of the difficulty and importance to him of opening the ship's safe–in which he claimed to have eventually found but a few shillings in cash. Among the goodies in the strong room, however, he did mention finding six million dollars in new Malay currency in transit to the Bank of Singapore–but of tea-sets, he says nothing.

Thames House and its forerunners always enjoy happy endings to their stories; and so Mrs. Ferguson's tale bears a glowing finish. She became a POW with her husband. However, on reaching Germany the authorities separated them and transferred her to Liebenau Internment Camp close to the Swiss Border and near to Lake Constance. These are proven facts.

Prisoners chosen by the relevant German authorities for exchange or repatriation would often be assembled in the Liebenau camp to await developments. Here she is said to have enjoyed tea parties with her beloved tea-set until 1943, when finally her repatriation to Britain occurred. She left Germany, but without her infamous tea-set. Violet became reunited with her husband in 1945 subsequent to his release from internment. That is also a proven fact.

However, the story continues that the Kriegsmarine had meanwhile carefully stowed her tea-set in a naval warehouse in Hamburg until the day it could be reunited with its owner. And so they eventually were reunited, and they lived in chip-free ceramic bliss happily ever after–and thus the story ends.

Perhaps an elegantly dressed, dapper gentleman speaking with a soft Scottish accent handed it to her as he introduced himself as, 'Bond ... James Bond'?

I think that's enough about the tea-set story, it could be true, or it could be a fiction. If the latter, why then should MI6 wish to concoct such a story?

Perhaps for the same reason the government wished to conceal from Australia and New Zealand *Automedon's* loss to a raider, together with the possible capture of the Far East Appreciation.

Even until 1948, when the intended recipient of the package (Brooke Popham) asked 'where was his copy', of the document and what had happened to it? Squadron-Leader Wiles, the then secretary of the Joint Chief of Staff Committee informed him that *Automedon* had been lost to a U-boat while on passage and had gone down together with the letter intended for his eyes alone.

Wiles was reputed to have said in his letter to Brooke-Popham that the circumstances surrounding the incident of its loss were not clarified until after Germany's fall. A clever ploy, and one that prevented Brooke-Popham from further questioning the false U-boat claim–always providing there were no leaks from other sources.

In 1941, seven years beforehand however, *Automedon's* 4th Engineer, Sam Harper, successfully reached home following his escape. He had recounted the true story of what had happened to *Automedon* in a series of official briefings. The government thereby knew of *Automedon's* fate, but persisted with recounting the U-boat lie until long after the war had ended.

There are no official papers available to the public that refer to discussions at any level in the British Government concerning the loss of *Automedon's* top-secret cargo.

And why shouldn't Australia and New Zealand know that Churchill was willing to lose Hong Kong, Malaya and Singapore to Japan should she enter the war in 1940?

In November of that year, the Royal Air Force had just won the Battle of Britain, but Britain's land forces remained depleted and under strength following its losses only a few weeks beforehand at Dunkirk. The threat of German invasion from across the Channel still loomed large. To Churchill and the cabinet, the security of the Empire and Dominions took a secondary priority to the defence of the Motherland.

The defence of Britain's Far East possessions required the deployment of extensive naval forces. Churchill did not have them at his disposal until they had defeated the Italian fleet in the Mediterranean, and only then could they be diverted to the Far East?

Should the governments of Australia or New Zealand come into possession of this knowledge they would inevitably feel increasingly threatened by Japan. As a consequence of which, they would likely withdraw their troops that were currently fighting Rommel in North Africa in order to strengthen their home defence. And Churchill needed those troops to remain active in the North African theatre to ensure the possibility of victory there. He could not risk the likelihood of their earlier withdrawal until Rommel had been defeated and Egypt and the Suez canal secured from his threat.

But that is another unproven supposition, albeit one that is upheld by a number of distinguished academics.

* * *

Automedon's ship's company now found themselves housed as prisoners of war aboard *Atlantis*. Once all were checked on board, they were lined up to face their old ship while the scuttling charges placed by Rogge's demolition officer, Leutnant Fehler, were exploded, and *Automedon* sank to the seabed. Many of her old crew turned their backs on the sight of their ship's final moments.

The following picture is taken from the Stern newspaper. It included an article from Dr. Goebbels Propaganda Ministry extolling the achievements of a lone German raider operating freely in the southern oceans without home support and successfully evading detection by Germany's enemies.

It is an article that much displeased Capt. Rogge, who always tried his level best to remain wraithlike and anonymous while waging his brand of warfare in these vast and uncrowded waters.

Fresh water replenishment always existed as a major problem for him. With a crew and captive complement totalling at times over 600 souls water consumption had to be strictly controlled. The nearest free supply where *Atlantis* might replenish her tanks and still remain undiscovered by Allied forces and other shipping lay on the French island of Kerguelen, an isolated islet lying on the very edge of Antarctica. The island had once been an important whaling station, but now as then, it lay abandoned and uninhabited.

Atlantis tended to resupply herself whenever her needs arose by capturing tankers and refrigerated vessels to replenish her bunkers and storerooms, and she proved to be extremely successful in doing this. On the few occasions when she could not wholly resupply herself, the German Navy's supply network of vessels would succour her. On a number of occasions *Atlantis* played her own part in this supply network, often refuelling and supplying the larger German surface vessels and U-boats operating in the oceans of the southern hemisphere.

Ships captured intact by *Atlantis* were despatched to wait at specified points in the south Indian Ocean, and there to wait for further orders. There were two such congregation points used by Rogge: 'Mongease' 300 miles south of the equator and close to the secondary station, Point 'Roton' at 03:30S::093:15E.

Whenever a captured vessel had outlived its usefulness to Rogge, he would transfer their crews aboard Atlantis and despatch their ship to the ocean floor.

* * *

Frank tells us in his notes that they were individually interviewed and searched soon after boarding Atlantis. Items of so-called contraband and value were taken from them in exchange for Third Reich promissory receipts.

Then they were assembled on deck and lined up as a group for photographing–'officers, ratings, passengers and the ship's cat too, had it managed to board a boat.'

I have been unable to find a picture for the *Automedon* photograph, but the following is of one taken onboard *Pinguin*, another raider. It is of the passengers and crew of the ships she had attacked during November 1940 and included *Nowshera* and *Maimoa*, British India and Shaw Savill and Albion Company vessels.

Frank recalled that the food and conditions on board *Atlantis* weren't too bad. They were always hungry, and strict water rationing proved to be a burden they had to get used to, but they were let out into the fresh air often and they were treated with respect, on the whole. Frank said: 'If we treated them with respect, we mostly got it back.'

Captive British seamen and passengers. Taken aboard 'Pinguin", November 1940 *Photo courtesy of RussDunshea (russdunshea89@wix.com/escapes)*

They were given a small tobacco and cigarette ration. He reckoned, 'It could've been a more generous allowance since they had taken two and a half million Chesterfields from us that we didn't know we had on board. And it was us, after all, who helped shift 'em onto *Atlantis*.'

* * *

Frank often said through a wry grin, 'Captain Rogge encouraged us to do sports and pastimes. Boxing was one of his favourites. He'd walk among us with Ferry, his little terrier that had become the ship's mascot, and talked to us. He'd answer any reasonable question as best he could. We got to trust him a bit. He became highly regarded by us for his fair play and sense of humanity. He didn't come across as a jackboot stamping Nazi at all.

'But one thing he would never do was allow boxing bouts between Germans and Brits. However much we asked him for one, he always said, 'No.' A fight between Germans and Norwegians was okay, and we could fight Norwegians or anybody else, but not the Germans. We supposed it was because *'Norskies'* were now considered by them to be like Germans, since their country had been occupied and was now run from Berlin.

'We had all the fresh air we wanted, but were battened down whenever she attacked other ships. While we were on board she added three more ships to her tally, and quite a few more of us to her bank of prisoners. It was starting to get a bit crowded now.'

Frank described Captain Rogge as a gentleman. He looked after them as well as he could and he held the respect of all on board. He would talk openly to everybody as he walked with his little terrier around the deck.

'Sprightly little thing, loved by all–well most of us: you've always got the miseries around you. I mean you get them everywhere you go. You know what I mean?'

* * *

The author wishes to acknowledge the cartoonist for this work and advice of his several and unsuccessful attempts to locate the copyright holder to seek his permission. The author will gladly apportion any caption the copyright holder might wish to be attached to this work should the copyright holder contact the author

'One day, Rogge found a bloke doing a sketch and suggested he start an art class. Can you imagine suggesting to some of them 'old salts' we had with us, them who had served their time on square-riggers, that they should start an *art class*?

'Beggars the imagination how they might go about it?'

Frank added: 'We were on board *Atlantis* for about a month before she got to be so overcrowded they had to move us on. They called up another of their captive ships, the Norwegian tanker *'Storstad'*. She had to take us on board and deliver us to wherever we had to go to next.'

* * *

'Never could any of us have imagined the consequences that would follow for the world at the end of next year because of us carrying that green canvas envelope and Capt. Ewan not managing to throw it overboard before the Germans attacked us. The Japanese were extremely grateful to this lowly sea-raider captain for the information inside it. They presented him with a Katana, their highest military honour. Only two other Germans had ever received this award–Goering and Rommel.'

Katana *License CCO Public Domain. Grateful thanks to Kai Stachowiack*

***

Atlantis had lived a charmed existence, but the end finally came to her and her exploits in 1941. She had been ordered to refuel U-68 in the South Atlantic and then proceed north of Ascension Island to replenish U-126.

Bletchley code breakers had picked up their rendezvous messages, and the Admiralty sent *HMS Devonshire* to meet them.

On 22nd November 1941 *Devonshire* arrived to find *Atlantis* in the process of refuelling U-126, and with the U-boat captain allegedly on board the raider taking a shower. U-126's 1st Lieutenant immediately took command. He cast off the hose and dived the U-boat, leaving an oil trace behind as she slipped away beneath the surface.

Atlantis got underway in an attempt to draw *Devonshire* south. Capt Oliver RN, commander of the *Devonshire* stayed well out of range of *Atlantis's* firepower.

From ten miles range, Oliver's first salvo straddled Atlantis. *Devonshire* had found the range and Rogge wrote in his memoir that he knew the game was up. He set smoke screens and ordered Lt. Fehler, his demolition officer, to set scuttling charges and ordered abandon ship as the next shells from *Devonshire* penetrated the smoke screen and landed on target.

Kapitan Rogge soulfully expressed his gratitude to Captain Oliver for having ordered delayed action fuses fitted to his shells. He wrote in his memoir:

'It showed the humanity of *Devonshire's* commander in his wish to minimize human casualties'

Had he set on-contact fuses the injuries and loss of life from shrapnel would have been unthinkable. Rogge scuttled *Atlantis* and his crew took to the boats.

It was the end of a tour of duty of 655 consecutive days in which they had destroyed twenty-two ships totalling 145,960 Gross Register Tons (GRT).

Atlantis burning and her crew clearing the **scene** *Photo Courtesy of Eduardo Montigonis Photos*

Captain Oliver on *Devonshire* remained acutely aware of the possibility of a submarine attack from U-126 and from any other U-boats making for the rendezvous with *Atlantis*. He kept the cruiser moving and dare not stop to rescue survivors. U-68 was still around. Her logbook recorded having fired a torpedo at *Devonshire* that had missed its target. *Devonshire* decided to leave the survivors to their fate. She lowered her battle ensign and triumphantly departed the scene.

And records show that the subsequent evacuation of Atlantis' survivors lost not a single man, a remarkable achievement. U-boats in the vicinity had surfaced and towed the Atlantis' lifeboats clear of the danger area until another team of four Italian submarines and four other German U-Boats organised by the Kriegsmarine had assembled and taken all 366 men on board of those cramped and tiny submarines, and then delivered them safely to Nantes in German Occupied France.

I regret there is no information regarding the fate of Rogge's terrier, 'Ferry'.

It is believed that the commander of U-126 later faced a disciplinary tribunal for abandoning his command during an engagement, and was severely censured as a consequence. Such is the price of a shower for a submariner when engaged on an active service patrol.

Hitler awarded Rogge the oak leaves to his Knight's Cross–Germany's highest award, the equivalent of awarding him a Victoria Cross twice.

Atlantis' survivors under tow. *Photo courtesy of Eduardo Montigonis Photos*

Rogge eventually went back to sea as commander of the heavy cruiser *Prinz Eugen*. He became the only German officer of Flag rank not arrested by the allies to face criminal charges at the end of the war.

Bathroom Delights at Milag. *A cartoon by Leslie Lace for Frank Walker Courtesy of the estate of Frank Walker*

INTERNATIONAL DEVELOPMENTS:

Japan craved to possess the Far Eastern colonies of France, Holland, Britain and America, but dared not move on them for fear of having to face two enemy naval forces in reprisal–the fleets of the United States of America and Great Britain.

With embarrassing haste, Hitler made a gift of the *Automedon* documents to Japan. They instantly served to remove Admiral Yamamoto's fears of reprisal from Britain should he attack the US fleet in Hawaii, and set him to work on his grand plan to bring this about. As a preliminary step, Japanese forces moved unopposed into Siam and Indo-China, ostensibly as advisers; where they promptly set about constructing and equipping air force bases. A little over a year later Japan attacked Pearl Harbour.

The day after that callous attack, their Siam based aircraft sank *HMS Prince of Wales* and *HMS Repulse* with horrendous loss of life in the South China Sea. At that time, these two capital ships effectively comprised the British Far East Fleet. Japan was now on the military move and turned what had until then been a purely European conflict into the Second World War.

Frank, and his shipmates, in bringing their vessel unknowingly into close quarters with the *Atlantis* had brought it on–and save for the master, they would have known nothing about the secret documents they had carried on board: papers that fell into enemy hands as a consequence and precipitated Japan's entry into the war.

It is why we can say, with tongues in cheeks, that the work product of sixteen year-old Frank Walker and his crewmates, in bringing *Automedon* into close proximity with the *Atlantis* on that day effectively caused the Second World War.

To be more historically accurate, it might be said that the failure of the War Cabinet's, Sir Cyril Newall in organising the dispatch of his document by a more secure means than an elderly cargo vessel, and to a slightly lesser extent, its master's failure to jettison the envelope when *Atlantis* first threatened his ship, hastened the entry of Japan into what became as a result, the Second World War.

From 'War Illustrated', courtesy of David Hearn.

CAPTIVITY AT SEA:

We last left Frank and his surviving shipmates being ferried by a convoy of motorboats into captivity aboard the German raider, *Atlantis*.

Frank and his fellows spent a month aboard *Atlantis* where he said they lived in a fairly amicable environment and suffered a reasonably comfortable time on board; especially so when one considers the reason for their presence on the raider. The food, while not plentiful, he said proved sufficient, although strict rationing applied to fresh water consumption.

While held aboard the raider, the ship's companies of five more vessels joined the throng held there in custody. They included the crew's of the *Port Brisbane*, *Port Wellington* and the British and India Company ships, *Norshera* and *Maimoa*.

The painting of the *Pinguin's* attack on *Maimoa* is by Australian artist Les Cowle, who painted it for *Maimoa's* Third Engineer, Russ Dunshea, also held captive with Frank aboard the *Atlantis*.

Russ, however, became one of five who escaped from the train the Germans had commandeered to transport the prisoners to Germany after their landing in France. Russ Dunshea eventually made it home following a harrowing trek through France and Spain.

The attack depicted in the painting portrays a favoured method of assault employed by all of the German surface raiders; each being equipped with either an Arado 196 or a Heinkel seaplane. The raider would approach disguised as a friendly merchant vessel. When close it would reveal its true self by hoisting its Nazi battle ensign and by showing its guns, while at the same time calling for the master to stop and to send no messages. Should the victim show signs of fleeing, the raider would launch its seaplane and strafe the decks and the amidships housing with the aircraft's machine guns as a discouragement to flight.

Two crewmen died following the strafing of the *Maimoa*. It might have been worse had 4th Engineer Dig Howlett not fired at the seaplane with a .303 Lee-Enfield rifle and scored a hit on its fuel tank–necessitating the aircraft's abandonment of its attack and an immediate return to *Pinguin*.

The German crews were well practiced in the swift recovery of these aircraft, and worked with a precision similar to that seen in today's

Formula 1 pit-crews. It took little time for a raider to swerve and flatten the sea to enable the seaplane to land safely alongside, where the ship's crew would be stood ready to fix a harness and lift it from the water into secure stowage on board ship.

Should a victim still not yield to the raider's orders, or alternatively, attempt to transmit an 'RRR- I am being attacked by a raider' warning message, the next step would be for the 'Q' ship to open fire with its 5.9 inch guns and shell its victim at close range. This is precisely what the records show as happened to *Automedon*.

Unlike U-boats, that might take only the captains and chief engineers on board from their kills, raiders would take whole crews aboard as POW's, and berth them until their numbers became too numerous and difficult for the ship to maintain and manage. At which point, the raider would call for a rendezvous with a support ship in order to offload them.

Frank had spent one day short of a month on *Atlantis* before being transferred with his captive comrades to a Kriegsmarine supply ship, *M.V. Storstad.*

Pinguin's attack on 'Maimoa', November 1940, Painting by Les Cowle. *Reproduced courtesy Russ Dunshea (dunshea89.wixsite.com/dunshea-escapes1941)*

M.V. STORSTAD:

M.V. Storstad *Courtesy of Wikipedia Commons Licence (CCO)*

Blytheswood Shipbuilding of Scotstoun had built the 8898 GRT, tanker *'Storstad'* earlier in 1940 for Norwegian owners, Kirkenes.

Atlantis' sister raider, *Pinguin*, had captured her fully laden with a cargo of diesel oil and kerosene. Now under German command and control, and being used as a unit in the German Navy's warship replenishment at sea programme. She also served as a prison ship for offloading the raiders' captives, holding them on board until ordered to a port, usually Bordeaux, to disembark them into imprisonment ashore.

Frank now lived as a Prisoner of War with 318 other seafarers taken from a number of Allied ships. On 8th December 1940, *M.V. Storstad* came alongside *Atlantis* and they were all moved into her.

The below is another picture of Frank's discharge book. Note that it's made up from his very first entry into the Merchant Navy in 1939 and also until the time of *Automedon's* capture: which, incidentally, is also the day he would have gone off pay under the prevailing practice of those times.

The page displays a hand-written entry of Frank as a Prisoner Of War. This particular entry, however, would have been executed only after he had returned to the UK and seafaring subsequent to his release from captivity at the end of the war. The Germans would not have made this entry.

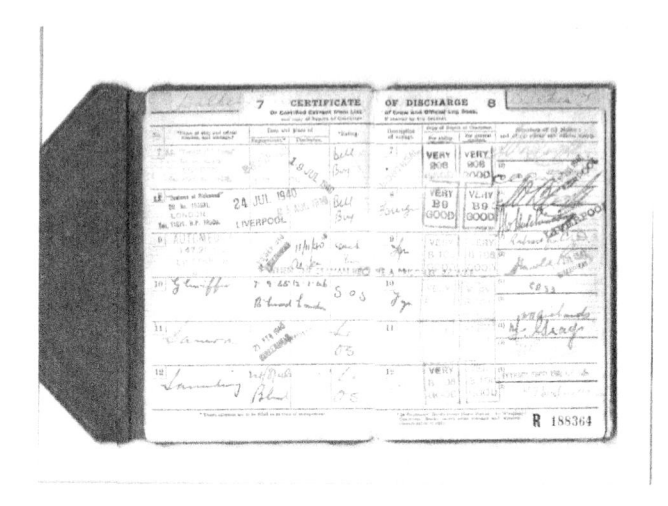

Inner pages of Frank Walker's Discharge 'A' Book
Courtesy of the estate of Frank Walker.

It rekindles the perplexing question posed earlier in this account. How can it be that Frank had possession of his original Discharge Book during his incarceration in Germany, and thus able to bring it home at the end of the war?

I will outline my thoughts on the matter a little later in this account.

Storstad accommodated its prisoners in roughly made dormitory areas rigged in the fo'c'sle and the forward dry cargo hold. These spaces provided poorly ventilated lodgings affording scant natural light, with no windows or scuttles set in the ship's side.

A rudimentary in-series single wire power system provided the only illumination to these rough and ready made quarters. The Germans held over them the threat of switching off the lighting, and to leave the men in permanent darkness as a condition for their good behaviour.

The sanitary provisions were also primitive, and consisted of a number of open, 40-gallon drums placed inside their accommodations. These would be hoisted out and emptied overboard each day. Men made for their own privacy arrangements and would sneak away with tins or containers of sufficient capacity into which a captive would perform his function and then deposit the residue into one of the open oil-drums. Conditions were primitive and basic, Air-Wick type fresheners and double layered soft tissues were unavailable–let us leave the subject there.

Taking the air on Storstad. That's a Spandau machine-gun barrel in the foreground *Photo courtesy of the estate of Frank Walker and its personal arrangement with Ambassador Eiji Seki.*

Below decks, washing or showering facilities were also unavailable. Strict fresh water rationing prevailed and was for drinking only. The men were each restricted to half a cup of drinking water a day. Men had to wash themselves and their clothing in salt water whenever operational opportunities allowed during their regular outings on deck. Food quality had deteriorated to poor, and with portions always provided in short measure. Every eleven days the men received an issue of vitamin pills.

Fresh air visits on deck were limited to one hour per man, twice a day.

The rudimentary lighting of their living spaces came under strict time control. Lights went out at 2000 each evening, but one exception to this rule applied on Christmas Day when they were allowed to enjoy an extra hour of its pale yellow illumination. Discipline, although not harshly applied was, nevertheless, strictly enforced. On the whole Frank conceded they were reasonably well treated, as long as they behaved themselves. Frank did manage to fall foul of one guard, a 'Bolshie' Petty Officer called Beckriche. Frank quickly learned that to enjoy a quiet life on board he had to keep out of this man's field of view.

Fresh air for one hour twice a day, but the washing can stay longer. *Photo courtesy of the estate of Frank Walker*

With nothing to do during a 22-hour per day confinement to their quarters, life soon became empty and basic for the captives. Tensions mounted, fuelled by the uncertainty of what might lie ahead of them. At this early stage of the war, Germany remained in the ascendancy.

Adding to their fears of survival grew the knowledge that the Royal Navy and Royal Australian Navy were actively hunting the oceans in pursuit of *Atlantis* and her ilk. The men knew that on finding a raider, allied warships would not hesitate to sink her–possibly killing her crew and her prisoners in whatever process might be deemed necessary to ensure the vessel's immediate destruction.

In spite of occasional threats by a few bullying German seafarers, fear of attack by a British warship remained the internees biggest worry.

In the ten weeks the seamen remained aboard *Storstad* the awfulness of their conditions and prospects proved too much for one Chinese seaman who committed suicide by jumping overboard while exercising during a periodic deck outing. One other British seaman also died of pneumonia during Frank's time on *Storstad*.

Carols broadcast over the ship's public address system marked Christmas Day on *Storstad*. Each captive gratefully received a gift of one bottle of beer and two extra cigarettes. All on board then spent a convivial day in which British and Germans looked beyond their national differences and exchanged seasonal good wishes.

* * *

Not knowing where they were on the world's oceans added to the prisoners' unease. Second Officer Phil Beehan, late of Port Line's steamship, *Port Wellington*, made an improvised sextant and compass card from a volume of Nicholl's Concise Guide that he had included among the personal possessions he had brought with him. Using a wristwatch and an old atlas he managed to fix their latitude and plot the various courses taken by *Storstad*.

His calculations proved to be quite accurate, in spite of the difficulty of having to take his sights through a crack in the hatch coaming, and conceal his doings from their watchful captors.

He correctly estimated their position on Christmas Day to be at fifty-five miles south of Cape Agulhas, the southernmost point of South Africa. And thereafter, he delivered quite accurate assessments of their journey northward to Bordeaux.

In the New Year they sailed into the South Atlantic Ocean. The POW's became better organised on board for exercise and social events, despite the restrictions placed upon them regarding access to the fo'c'sle head and the foredeck. Hunger and thirst remained their main problem throughout their time on board and the principal subject of their conversations.

* * *

On 3rd January 1941 all prisoners were ordered on deck to witness the *Storstad's* rendezvous with the *Admiral Scheer*, the German heavy cruiser of the *Deutschland* class.

Admiral Scheer in Gibraltar, 1936 *Photo courtesy of Wikipedia Commons*

Storstad had a responsibility in the German logistics chain to resupply and bunker the warship whenever called upon to do so: she had been captured loaded with a full cargo of diesel oil and kerosene.

The POW's benefited from the cruiser's own piracy for she provided them in return with a plentiful supply of Fray Bentos corned beef, and not so fresh eggs taken from a luckless merchantman the Admiral Scheer had encountered and attacked prior to their rendezvous.

It proved to be quite a surprise when the *Scheer's* dentist visited the tanker during the rendezvous and set about extracting any painful or bad teeth that were bothering the prisoners. In spite of him being an ardent Nazi, the dentist proved to be a highly skilled dental surgeon, and his patients suffered little pain while undergoing his treatments: notwithstanding their being no anaesthetic available to ease the discomforts of his procedures.

With rare exceptions, mutual respect continued to prevail between the British and Germans, in spite of them being adversaries at war.

* * *

Unable to work in England as a doctor, Karel Sperber had accepted employment as a ship's purser. But his medical knowledge and skills came in very good use on *Storstad*, and with other prisoners with whom he later shared his period of captivity.

Doctor Karel Sperber. *Though this image is subject to copyright, its use is covered by the U.S. fair use laws, and the stricter requirements of Wikipedia's non-free content policies, because: # It is a historically significant photo of a famous individual. # It is of much lower resolution than the original. Copies made from it will be of very inferior quality. # The photo is only being used for informational purposes. And to allow recognition of the subject from the text that follows # Its inclusion in the article adds significantly to the following text because the photo and its historical significance are the object of discussion in the article.*

When they arrived at Bordeaux, the Germans separated him from his *Automedon* shipmates because of his Jewish religion. Instead of eventually going on to Marlag with them, the Gestapo sent him to Auschwitz-Birkenau for his internment. There he survived five years of dreadful ordeal that included the infamous death march to Gleiwitz and thence on to Buchenwald concentration camp.

During his time in Auschwitz, the camp commandant forced Dr. Sperber to assist the infamous *Schutzstaffel* (SS) physician, Carl Clauberg with his sterilization experiments, performed unwillingly on as many as 400 Jewish women. After the war, Dr. Sperber provided valuable and detailed testimony to the War Crimes Commission against those guilty of these crimes.

The Red Army had captured Clauberg in 1945. After a fair trial at Nuremberg in 1946, where the court found him guilty of his crimes and sentenced Clauberg to 25 years imprisonment. He died in 1957.

Those who knew Dr. Sperber as a purser on *Automedon* described him as a quiet, respectful and well-organised officer. During his internment he treated many inmates, using his skill and ingenuity to treat life-threatening conditions with nothing more than his bare hands and his knowledge.

He eventually returned home to his wife who had waited for him in London, where in 1946, the King had him whisked off to Buckingham Palace to adorn him with the OBE for his services to prisoners of war.

He returned to sea eventually as a ship's doctor, and then later, for a time, he worked for the Ceylon administration, but by then he had contracted Hodgkinson's disease and he passed away in 1957, aged only 47.

Do you remember we talked earlier of Frank having his discharge book in his possession throughout his internment?

Knowing something of the background from which Dr. Sperber had escaped in German occupied Czechoslovakia, and his awareness of the importance of paperwork to everyday life in oppressive regimes, my guess is this: the good doctor would have used part of his 15–minute time allowance to gather his personal possessions prior to quitting *Automedon* to include in his baggage the discharge books of all those on board. As the ship's purser, they would, after all, have been in his safe keeping on the ship.

But that is only an unsubstantiated assumption expounded in an attempt to explain how Frank, and the others from Automedon, had possession of their discharge books while they were held in German captivity.

I am honoured to mention Doctor Sperber OBE in this account as yet an additional memorial to yet another worthy and wonderful man of the Golden Generation. May he rest in peace!

BORDEAUX:

Map by R Botev *Attribution Wikipedia commons license* CC-BY-SA-3.0

A sound knowledge of the changes to national boundaries would be essential for any prospective escapees.

And escape was already brooding in the minds of some of those confined on board the *Storstad* even before she had arrived in Bordeaux.

German patrols in Bordeaux, 1941 *Reproduced courtesy Russ Dunshea (dunshea89.wixsite.com/dunshea-escapes1941.Wikipedia Commons licence*

On disembarking with wobbly legs after eighty days at sea, Frank noticed the river under continuous patrol by German destroyers, and with army squads incessantly patrolling the streets of the city of Bordeaux. Security was tight.

69

The men had little opportunity for sightseeing however, for no sooner had they disembarked from *Storstad* than they were herded into cattle trucks and entrained to FRONT STALAG 21, a prison camp located in a suburb of Bordeaux, at St. Médard-en-Jalles sixteen kilometres to the northwest of the city centre.

Here they came up against an administrative hurdle of having to apply an official definition to these incomers. There were no ready rules for these officials to consult regarding foreign seamen brought in from their ships for no other reason than them being crewmen serving aboard their ship at the time of its capture by German forces.

Merchant Navy crews serving at sea during World War Two were essentially unarmed volunteers, and were thus properly classed as civilians. As such, they were not subject to military law and were not, strictly speaking, entitled to the rights of prisoners of war under the Geneva Convention. Those non-existent rights, therefore, placed no internationally binding obligation on the captor to feed these detainees.

The Germans at St. Médard, however, took a sensible view and treated their seafarer captives as POW's, which gave them daily comestibles, but to their detriment also denied them the opportunity of an early repatriation–as enjoyed by the women passengers and other bona fide civilians taken from ships by the Kriegsmarine.

Therefore, no foreseeable prospect of early freedom lay in short-term for the *Storstad's* human cargo. And this collective awareness resulted in depression and despair weighing heavily upon the men, which in turn fostered in a number of them an urgent desire to be free, that prompted the emergence of plans to escape home through France's neighbouring, neutral countries.

In this their first camp, the imprisoned seamen endured a uniform and unvarying daily diet of thin vegetable soup, accompanied by a small lump of bread and ersatz coffee: this to provide them with their bodily sustenance. Activity during their days consisted of milling around in clusters and playing football. Books in English were rare to find and chess sets had to be hand carved from whatever scrap materials they could find.

Barbed wire and machine guns guarded the camp, and in this soul destroying, environment, where boredom ruled their days, tempers frayed easily and often. Despondency set in, and with it, desperation followed closely behind to torment them. The new prisoners had some limited contact with a few French locals who came into the camp to make occasional repairs, and from whom those contemplating escape sought to learn how far from the camp, and in which direction to lay a course to the closest section of the border with Free Vichy France.

* * *

Picture reproduced by kind permission of Wrestling Heritage.com. Text and comments below the image attributed to Paul Rabinowitz, Harry's grandson.

The human hauls of German surface raiders brought some interesting people together in their captivity. One of whom included ex-professional wrestler, Harry Rabin. In his day Rabin had been a world champion contender for wrestling honours, and enjoyed respect and celebrity on the major wrestling circuits.

He also became well known around the London docklands, where he would often attend the meetings organized by British Communist Party General Secretary Harry Pollitt, and serve as the politician's bodyguard.

Rabin entered the POW net when *Port Brisbane,* the ship where he had worked as a coal trimmer, became a victim of German raider *Pinguin*. Harry constantly had escape on his mind and in this endeavour he teamed up with *Automedon's* Liverpudlian 4th Engineer, Sam Harper. Together they opened an escape tunnel from beneath the St. Médard hospital building. Unfortunately, before they could complete their work they were moved on to Germany.

71

Washing of clothes and persons at St. Médard had to be done with cold, but, thankfully, with fresh water. They lived in huts accommodating up to a hundred persons, and slept on double tier bunks, but without mattresses.

On unannounced occasions a truck would arrive in the compound and tip a load of straw on the ground for them to make into pailliasses. There always followed a mad scramble for the straw when these trucks arrived. The more straw an inmate could grab, the softer would be his bunk for sleeping, for there would be nothing otherwise between an inmate's body and the bare wooden boards of his bunk. An issue of a single blanket completed a POW's bedding–there were no pillows, sheets or eiderdowns provided.

The men remained here for a month before being moved out and marched to the railhead for onward transit to Germany.

* * *

The war diary kept by Frank is truly a valuable item that he has handed down to us. These diaries were blank-page booklets issued by the YMCA to POW's in Germany through the facilities of the Swiss Red Cross. The idea being to provide encouragement for the men to occupy their minds during the bleak period of their internment by keeping a record of their experiences in words and sketches.

Frank had to wait until he arrived in Germany to collect his diary. However, as we leave him marching to the railhead on his way to Lower Saxony, it seems an appropriate place to show his opening page.

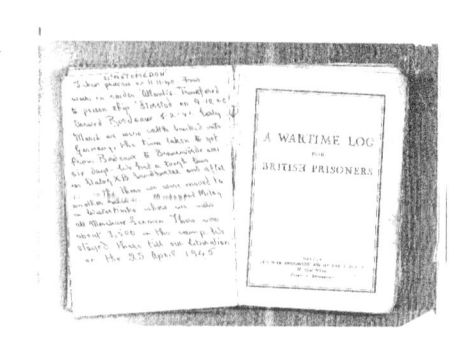

Courtesy of the estate of Frank Walker.

SANDBOSTEL:

Sketch attributed to Frank Walker *Courtesy of the estate of Frank Walker*

Onward to Germany!

Frank claims to have travelled to Germany in cattle trucks, while others on the train said they were transported in third class passenger wagons. Since five of Frank's ex-*Storstad* group escaped from the train on the journey, and in three unconnected adventures. I am inclined to go with their judgement. It is possible that the train comprised a variety of rolling stocks–the German guards surely would not have travelled in cattle trucks.

All five escapees who jumped from the train eventually reached home safely. But theirs are, perhaps, stories to tell on another day.

Back on the train, and after six days of travelling mostly through the night, it eventually delivered them to Sandbostel Stalag XB during the night hours.

They were fortunate that no recriminations were directed against them for the absence of the five men who had jumped from the train while en route there.

Sandbostel lies in Lower Saxony, and is located approximately twenty-five miles equidistant from Bremen and Hamburg. The men found on their arrival that they entered a site functioning as a joint military and internment camp. As the war progressed, Sandbostel gained for itself notoriety as a rather nasty concentration camp. Fortunately for Frank and his *ex-Storstad* shipmates, the British civilian seafarers had moved to another camp before the starvation, cruelty and death regimens had begun in earnest within the boundaries of Sandbostel camp.

The camp arrangement subdivided the inmates into separate sections housing differing nationalities. Confusion immediately followed once again regarding the status of civilian seamen who were not provided for by the Geneva Convention.

Their captors at Sandbostel insisted therefore, that no obligation fell on them to feed civilian captives, and made no attempt to do so. Luckily for Frank and the others who arrived there with him, the Swiss Red Cross proved to be extremely active in the region and swiftly sorted out that rather major problem.

Sandbostel Camp in 1943 (photographer unknown, courtesy and copyright of the International Committee of the Red Cross, V-P-HIST-03467-29A)

The two hutted British compounds were set up at the end of the main highway and adjacent to the French Algerian POW compound. Royal Navy personnel took the right compound and Merchant Navy personnel the left.

Sandbostel Camp (Photographer unknown, courtesy and copyright of the Frank Falla Archive and the International Committee of the Red Cross, V-P-HIST-03467-30A)

On arrival, the guards led the men into an administrative hut furnished only with a single, long table running down its centre. Onto its tabletop the seamen were compelled to place all of their remaining personal possessions. To their surprise and dismay, they then were made to undergo a thorough body search conducted by French POW's.

Frank was more than a little put out by the thoroughness with which the French carried out this task. All of their valuables were retained, for which they were again given worthless Third Reich stamped receipts in exchange.

Their hutted living quarters comprised of either, a long open plan hut with no subdivisions throughout its length, or a hut subdivided into twelve-man rooms arranged either side of a central corridor. There were no toilet or washing facilities provided inside the huts.

Men were allocated to a hut as they were marched in line through the camp. There were no provisions for segregating officers from ratings. The Germans were confused when asked to provide this separation. They couldn't understand the logic behind the request since the internees were all civilians and therefore of the same status: the question of rank should not arise among them.

Reproduced by kind permission of Falko Sieker of Lippefotos, 11 Nov 2023 *Creative Commons (CCO)*.

Nevertheless, in Teutonic thoroughness the guards responded positively to the request for segregation. They placed the officers in the twelve-roomed huts on the left hand side of the hut and ratings into those on the right side of the central aisle: but all still living together in the same huts. Problem solved.

This distinction did become important later, however, since ratings were obliged to work on non-military tasks in the German work *kommandos*, such as tree felling, peat digging and farm work. The Germans agreed with the British argument that officers and petty officers should not have to perform physical labour.

Until their feeding regime had finally been decided, the British contingent had to go hungry. Fortunately the Algerians in the neighbouring compound came to their rescue and fed the Britons from their meagre supplies of dates, grains and turnip gravy.

* * *

Frank found himself on defaulters for quite a lot of the time that he spent at Sandbostel, but only for minor indiscretions. Being both young and small his punishments often took the corporal form of those afforded to an unruly child in those days. Instead of suffering prison, or other more onerous penalties, the guards would slap him about his legs with their sword and bayonet scabbards.

Frank had once objected to working on 'Smelly Nelly', this being the outside and the only toilet for the detainees. Smelly-Nelly comprised of a simple arrangement of a horizontal pole placed at the requisite height across a deep hole in the ground. It worked with a movable timber covering to guard against adverse weather. Another hole would lie already dug for use beside it when the current latrine in use became filled, and then the structure would be moved bodily along to the new hole, and the old one backfilled with the local sandy earth. Notwithstanding his objections, Frank got to know Smelly-Nellies rather well during his remaining time in Germany, in both Sandbostel and Milag-Marlag Nord camps. But let's move on.

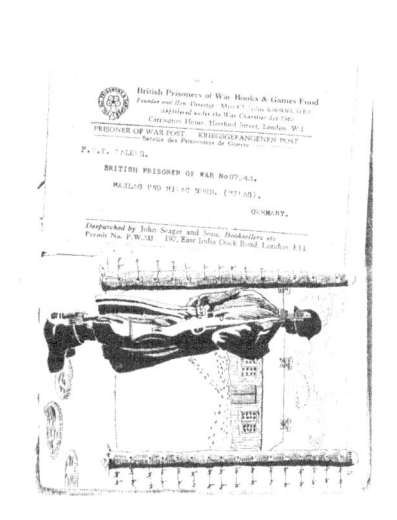

* * *

Address label from Seagar's Book Shop. *From Frank's War Diary, courtesy the estate of Frank Walker*

POW's were allowed to send out two letters a month through the Swiss Red Cross, and to receive unlimited numbers of letters from home. Frank at last received word from his Mum, and learned that she had moved to a permanent home in New Brighton.

He also received a book from Seagar's Bookshop in London's East India Dock Road, arranged for him and paid for by a little known charity run by the wonderful and redoubtable Miss Christina Knowles OBE: an aid organisation that provided books and games for British Prisoners of War.

The Licensed Victuallers Association had set up another, and similar fund for providing POW's with books and games. A number of their Monopoly Boards, however, were designed to incorporate special features in their structure that secreted silk maps and other tools to assist would be escapees. These 'doctored' sets were identified by a bright red dot placed in the 'GO' square.

Once the Red Cross had sorted out their feeding problem, the German camp authorities decided that the Algerians would remain responsible for giving food to the British seamen, and apportioned rations accordingly.

The Algerians cooked their meals in field kitchens and the daily menu invariably consisted of the inevitable turnip soup that displayed no signs of ever having been in contact with meat or grease, accompanied by a 200 gram piece of bread, or a single boiled potato.

'Peggies' from the British compounds were charged with collecting these precious rations from the Algerian compound at a set time each day.

The Germans considered food theft as a serious crime. Frank learned how serious on a day when he performed the chore of duty 'peggy'. He had collected from the Algerians the rations for the twenty-four men in his set. A French Algerian POW attempted to steal soup from the British allowance carried by Frank. The Algerian had dipped a can into Frank's bucket of soup as the boy passed him by.

A German guard had witnessed this attempted theft and retribution followed swiftly and finally to the man. With no call for an explanation, the guard shouted, 'Stoppen' at the man as he raised his rifle, and summarily shot the would-be thief dead. Frank returned to his hut with the bulging eyes of horror and disbelief after witnessing such a harrowing application of German drumhead justice.

Another similar incident occurred shortly afterwards, when the men went on strike for more rations. The POW doctors in the camp had approached the Germans for a greater food allowance on behalf of those men working on the heavier-labour work *kommandos*. Their request met with an instant refusal. The camp commandant would not even discuss the issue with the doctors. To gain consideration for their request, they returned to their huts and organised a strike of the workers under the maxim of –No food, no work.

The men refused to work the next day and milled around in a group, kicking their heels in the dust of the football pitch. After a few minutes of inertia from the camp administration, they heard the singing voices of approaching troops on the march. The sound grew in volume and stopped when a squad of German infantry pulled into the strikers compound and set up Spandau machine guns on tripods facing the strikers on the football pitch.

The young commandant then came out of his office, adjusted his uniform cap on his head and gave the men an ultimatum: one-minute to get to work–or else. There followed a mad scramble among the men to get to their work details. The commander, Kapitan Prisch, had appeared to be a decent chap until then, with scant traces of Nazism embracing his demeanour.

At an opportune moment some time later, the Senior British Officer asked him if he would have gone through with the execution of the men had they continued to refuse to go back to work?

'Of course,' he replied immediately and without any prior thought,

'You would have left me no choice. I would have lost my face had I conceded to their action and the doctor's demands for more, but non-existent food.'

Such is war and the burden of responsibility of command during its prosecution.

* * *

On another day, Frank managed to engineer himself onto the peat digging squad. They cut turves from a bog and stacked them in cones to dry. It proved to be hard and sweaty work. One day during a slack moment, Frank managed to creep inside one of the tall cones and promptly went to sleep. He stayed asleep when the detail finished work for the day and had returned to the camp–nobody had missed him. His workmates and the guards had left him there. He woke later and with a start realised what had happened. Once his initial panic had subsided, thoughts of escape crossed his mind, but were quickly dismissed. He had some ability in the German language by then, but not enough to pass himself off as a local. Besides, he had no idea of where he was in the country, much less of where he should head for or how he might get there. So he went back to the main gate where, horror of horrors, the guard would not believe his tale or let him come inside.

The guard had thought, because of the boy's youth and small size (4'4" in 1939) that Frank was a village kid and playing him a prank. Instead of opening the gate, he bellowed at the boy:

'Geh Weg! Geh nach hause zu deiner mutter!' – Go away, Go home to your Mum.'

The boy, fearful of where he might have to spend the night, held his own with the guard. He stuck out his jaw, rattled his POW dog tags at him and through tear filled eyes insisted that he lived inside the camp. With grumbles, the guard let him inside, but that ended Frank's employment on the peat digging detail. From then on, and for his remaining time at Sandbostel, he had to spend more time as a companion worker for Smelly Nelly.

* * *

As the war progressed towards its eventual conclusion the camp began over-filling with Russians and others. It evolved more into the hideous concentration camp it eventually did become. Typhus broke out in several of the less fortunate sections than those occupied by our boys. The Red Cross placed heavy pressure on the German authorities to move the Royal Navy and Merchant Navy contingents to another, more suitable location for them.

The Germans agreed quite quickly to this humanitarian request, but under a condition that the incumbents dismantle their present huts and reassemble them on a small ex-Luftwaffe training site at nearby Westertimkie.

The British seafarers readily agreed to the provision, and so the chippies in the group got back onto their tools. Towards the end of October 1941 the British sections slowly shifted themselves sixteen miles farther to the south of Sandbostel, and into cleaner air and open countryside. Frank had now celebrated his seventeenth birthday and he readily joined the others in the work of dismantling and reassembly of the huts in what was to become Milag-Marlag Nord, and his final home as a POW in Germany.

MILAG-MARLAG NORD:

Sketch of Frank, drawn by fellow POW 'Jeff'. The walk to Milag.
Courtesy of the estate of Frank Walker

Frank's war diary provides us with a concise record of his time spent at Milag. If you remember, we have already seen its opening page in the Bordeaux section of this account. From here, I think it better to let Frank tell you the rest of the story of his time there through the entries in his war diary–and in his own words, as far as possible. All yours, Frank!

'As we got the huts reassembled at Marlag, we had to march the sixteen miles there to go and live in them. We all left Sandbostel with no regrets, having found the place a nightmare.

'At first, we didn't appreciate the newer, more pleasant country surroundings. I suppose it was because food and the lack of it always preyed on our minds night and day.

'We had us a bigger Smelly-Nelly at Marlag'
Photographer unknown. Extract from Frank Walker's War Diary, courtesy of the estate of Frank Walker

'We still had the separate compounds for Royal Navy and Merchant Navy personnel. The RN were berthed at Milag, it stands for military. Their camp lay three hundred yards away from ours at Marlag, which stands for Maritime. The camp's proper name is Milag-Marlag Nord, but most if us just called it Milag.'

A 'levelling' experience for some of the more proud inmates. *Extract from the Frank Walker war diary, courtesy of the estate of Frank Walker*

'Milag at first proved to be a great levelling experience for some of us–especially for the big-ship captains who found they had to adjust their outlook and position to being equals with everybody else now they were POW's. It came down hard for some of them to get used to–but they had no choice in the matter.'

We all had nicknames. 'Titch and 'Winkle' were mine *Extract from the Frank Walker war diary, courtesy of the estate of Frank Walker*

'We didn't much use our real names when we talked to each other–we gave each other nicknames instead. 'Course, I'd brought mine with me!'

'We actually got paid for whatever work we did for Jerry, just like we did on *Atlantis*. Forty pfennigs a day was our pay, and they printed our own camp currency. There wasn't a lot to buy, but the camp money went well with those locals we came in contact with–they didn't have much either, poor beggars, but it came in useful for buying fags and other bits and pieces.

'Not all of the boys could make it through to the end, illness and disease took them, but we always held a proper funeral service for them that 'swam the channel.' A funeral always added a sombre note to a day, whenever it happened, 'cos it made you wonder ... would it be your turn next?

* * *

Frank extreme right, on a peat digging detail. *Photographer unknown. Extract from the Frank Walker war diary, courtesy of the estate of Frank Walker*

'We still had peat bogs to work at Milag and I found myself giving it another go on a digging detail for a time, but I never risked hiding inside a stacked peat cone again. That's me on the far right and front of the above photo.

'We were allowed to volunteer to be on different work details. At one time I fancied becoming an electrician, so I opted for that detail, only to find myself digging holes for power and telegraph poles.

'One time when I was out on a working party, they sent me off to somewhere with a message for another squad. I got lost and found myself entirely on my own, not knowing where I was, or where to go. I just walked until I came to a farmhouse and knocked on the door. I had a bit of German by then and explained my dilemma to the farmer's wife. It was getting late in the afternoon by now.

'With no fuss, the farmer's wife took immediate charge of the situation. She packed her man off on his bicycle to tell the camp where I was and for them to come and collect me. Meanwhile she packed me off upstairs into a bedroom with a proper bed and eiderdown for a bit of a sleep while we waited for the guards to come an' pick me up.

'After having a bit of a snooze, I wandered back downstairs. The guards hadn't yet appeared so she sat me down at their kitchen table and made me a sandwich from a huge lump of pure white fat with a thin line of red bacon running through it. I swear that was the best tasting bacon sandwich I have ever had–before or since.

'I was eating this lovely thing when the German guards arrived. They mistook me for the son of the house at first and went upstairs to look for the prisoner. Laugh! They left their rifles lying beside me at the table when they went upstairs.

'Back in the camp, they gave me a few more punishments because of this, some of which were very unpleasant indeed–like being taken out in a truck to pick up and handle dead bodies after the air raids. And as the war went on, the RAF tended to pop in a bit more often than when we first got here."

* * *

Footwear was always a problem for us *Extract from the Frank Walker war diary, courtesy of the estate of Frank Walker*

'Food and clothing continued to be major problems throughout all our time in the camps. Boots and shoes were just unobtainable. We had to make clogs or sabots out of bits of wood, and use scraps of cloth for socks.

'We did manage to get hold of some jackets and trousers–mostly they were old and captured French and Belgian army uniforms: some of which were heavily marked KGF on their backs. (KriegGeFangene = POW)

'Toward the end of the war one of the guys, Bill Chambers, I think was his name, got a bit more boots than he bargained for when he found out how severely the Third Reich dealt with unauthorised possession of food.

'He had stolen a single potato and got found out. Luckily he had a bit of a gift of the gab and said he'd found it on a road. Even so, they dragged him up before a civil criminal court that handed him down four months in gaol. I recalled that Algerian bloke at Sandbostel who got shot for only trying to nick some of our soup ration. By that token Bill was lucky.

He had to serve his time in a factory that recovered the usable leather from worn-out army jackboots. It was right up on the top floor of a Hamburg warehouse, and at that time the RAF's Lancaster and Halifax bombers were in the habit of visiting Hamburg on a daily basis. Luckily, he made it safely back into the compound at the end of his time.'

* * *

'There weren't many actual escape attempts from our camp. Two or three got away from the RN camp–it was in there where they worked the famous 'Albert RN' scam that's since got itself well known through TV. They all headed for Sweden whenever they made a break. There was always lots of talk about escape in our hut, but rarely did anything serious ever come of it, but the idea of us escaping kept Jerry nervous, and every now and then we'd get these notices given out to tell us 'Escape is no longer a Sport.' As if it ever was.'

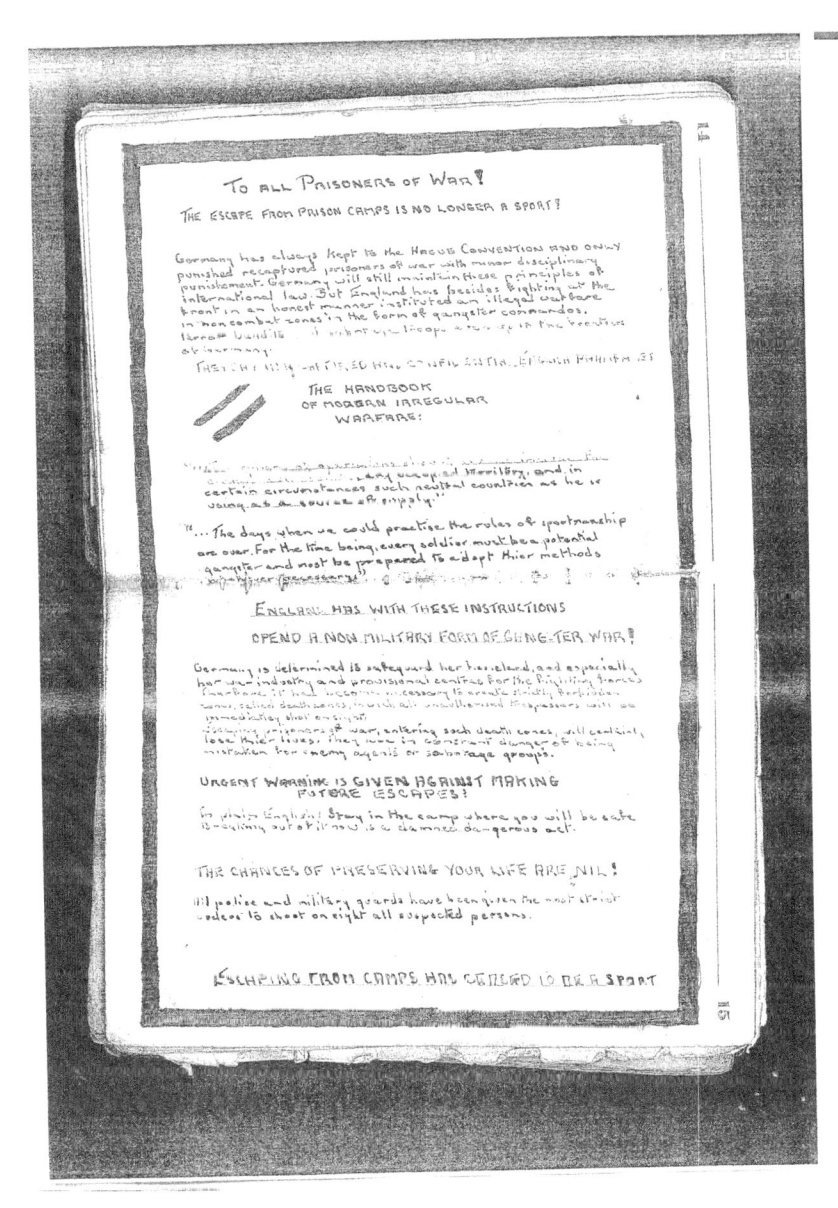

> **TO ALL PRISONERS OF WAR!**
>
> THE ESCAPE FROM PRISON CAMPS IS NO LONGER A SPORT!
>
> Germany has always kept to the Hague Convention and only punished recaptured prisoners of war with minor disciplinary punishment. Germany will still maintain these principles of international law. But England has besides fighting at the front in an honest manner instituted an illegal warfare in non combat zones in the form of gangster commandos. These bandits do what ye troops are up to the practice of leaving:
>
> THESE NEW UNITED STATES REGULATIONS ARE PUBLISHED IN
>
> ~~~ THE HANDBOOK
> OF MODERN IRREGULAR
> WARFARE:
>
> "... commands operations directly ... from occupied territory, and in certain circumstances such neutral countries as he is using as a source of supply."
>
> "... The days when we could practice the rules of sportsmanship are over. For the time being, every soldier must be a potential gangster and must be prepared to adopt their methods whenever necessary."
>
> ENGLAND HAS WITH THESE INSTRUCTIONS
>
> OPENED A NON MILITARY FORM OF GANGSTER WAR!
>
> Germany is determined to safeguard her homeland, and especially her war industry and provisional centres for the fighting forces. Therefore it has become necessary to create strictly forbidden zones, called death zones, in which all unauthorised trespassers will be immediately shot on sight.
>
> Escaping prisoners of war, entering such death zones, will certainly lose their lives. They are in constant danger of being mistaken for enemy agents or sabotage groups.
>
> URGENT WARNING IS GIVEN AGAINST MAKING
> FUTURE ESCAPES!
>
> To plain Englishy! Stay in the camp where you will be safe! Breaking out of it now is a damned dangerous act.
>
> THE CHANCES OF PRESERVING YOUR LIFE ARE NIL!
>
> All police and military guards have been given the most strict orders to shoot on sight all suspected persons.
>
> ESCAPING FROM CAMPS HAS CEASED TO BE A SPORT!

Escape is no longer a sport! As if it ever was? *Extract from the Frank Walker war diary, courtesy of the estate of Frank Walker*

* * *

The Searches! *Extract from the Frank Walker war diary, courtesy of the estate of Frank Walker*

'Every few weeks the local Gestapo would land on us and supervise the camp guards while they made them carry out a thorough search of the camp for contraband.

They were also paranoid about escapes. We supposed they lost 'smarty' points if one of us ever got away. We got pretty good at hiding things and found the best way to handle them was to let them find something minor, and then they would give up before they found something more important to us.

It usually meant one of us had to volunteer to spend a few days in the 'Kooler.'

* * *

"When?" How Much Longer?"

'Needless to say, getting home was always on our minds–every last one of us asked ourselves these questions every blinking day.'

"When will I get out of here?" "Will I ever go home?"

Will it ever end? *Extract from the Frank Walker war diary, courtesy of the estate of Frank Walker*

* * *

The Camp Theatre *Extract from the Frank Walker war diary, courtesy of the estate of Frank Walker*

'In a way we were lucky to have a Hollywood actor in the camp with us. Henry Mallinson had been a passenger on a Shaw Savill boat when it got itself captured, and they sent him along here to be with us until we got out.

'Jerry encouraged us to occupy our talents in theatrics rather than escapology, and Henry soon got the camp theatre up and running. We put on some good shows during our time there.

'Stan Hugill, a Liverpool lad and our helmsman off the *Automedon* at the time of our capture, found out he had a talent for writing and directing, but only after he got in the camp. He'd never done it before and it probably wouldn't have happened for him if he hadn't been in there.

'Although I say it myself, they were shows, good enough that people ashore would pay good money to go and see.

By the way ... Henry Mallinson's sister was the famous aviator, Amy Johnson, but laugh, she never had a mind to drop in on us.

* * *

'I loved this' *Extract from the Frank Walker war diary, courtesy of the estate of Frank Walker*

'Horse Racing! Now this was a big favourite of mine. We had our own horseracing club and I was a full and active member. We ran it with wooden horses and throws of the dice, just like we used to do at sea, and how Lennie and Peter do it every month still at Mariners' Park. Made myself a few bob some days–well, we called pfennigs bobs in the camp.'

* * *

We never lost our sense of humour *Extract from the Frank Walker war diary, courtesy of the estate of Frank Walker*

'We had a few good artists among us who made us all laugh by taking the 'Mickey' out of us with their cartoons, all good natured stuff. We mostly got on with each other because we had to. There was nothing to be gained by being at war with one another. Mind you, tempers did fray from time to time and a fight would get you a week in the Kooler.

* * *

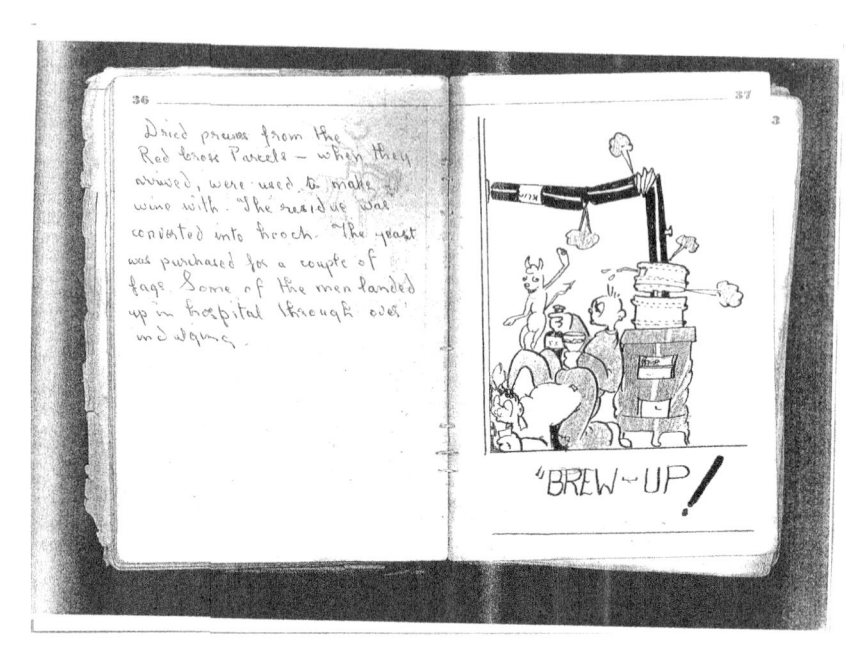

Wherever you get a bunch of seamen together... Extract from the Frank Walker war diary, courtesy of the estate of Frank Walker

'Wherever you get men herded together it will not be long before there's a still of sorts hidden and bubbling away. We put the prunes from the Red Cross parcels to good use this way and bought yeast from the locals for a few pfennigs. To get stuff like yeast we had to try to contact the locals when we were outside on work parties, or when they came into the camp to do repairs–but that was difficult. There were always guards watching what we were up to.

* * *

'I can't say enough that's good about the Red Cross parcels. We got 'em twice every month. Suffice it to say, they really did save lives.'

'Once things had settled down, we received mail from home quite regularly and then were allowed to send out two letters and four postcards a month. It was all done through the Red Cross and I was in touch with Mum again. She was pretty settled by now and quite at home in New Brighton. Writing letters to her and getting her replies had a settling effect on me. I started thinking about my future at home and what I might do when this lot was finally over.

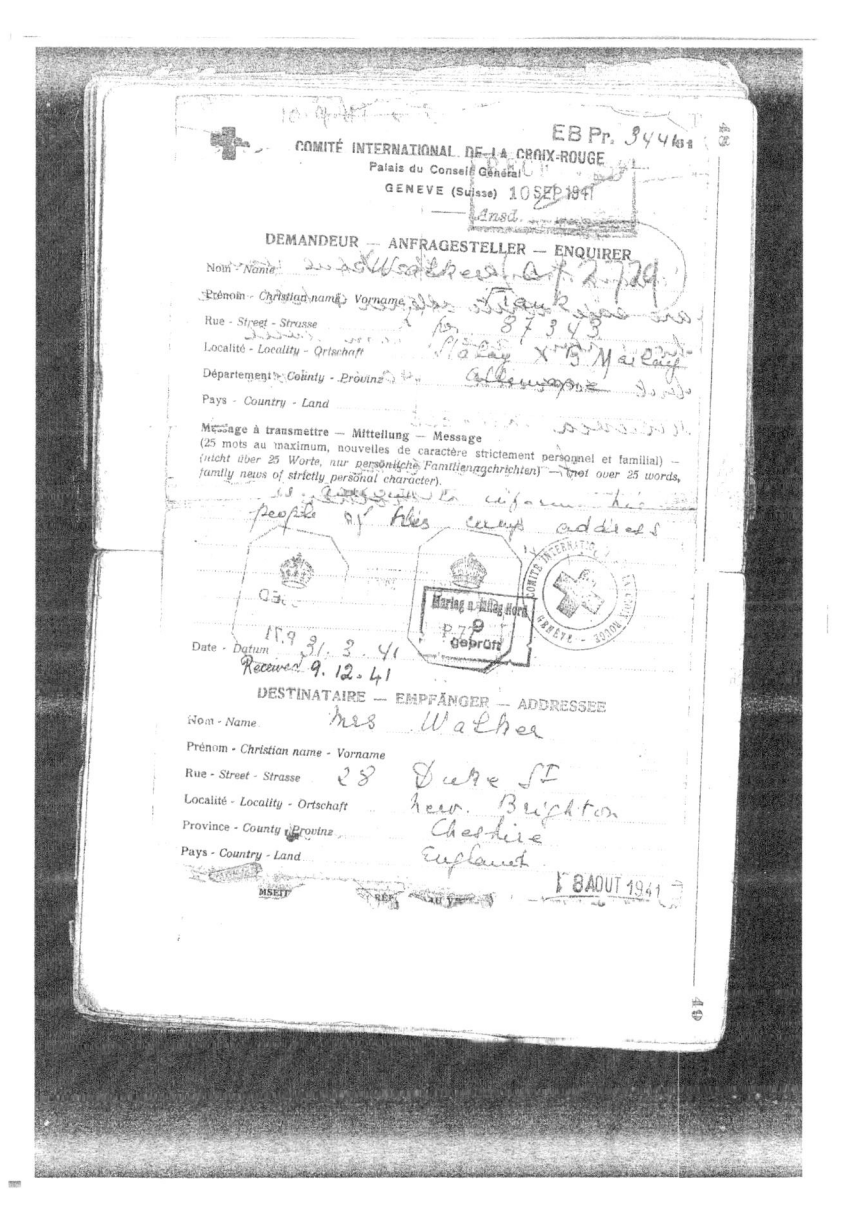

That 'wonderful' Swiss Red Cross. *Extract from the Frank Walker war diary, courtesy of the estate of Frank Walker*

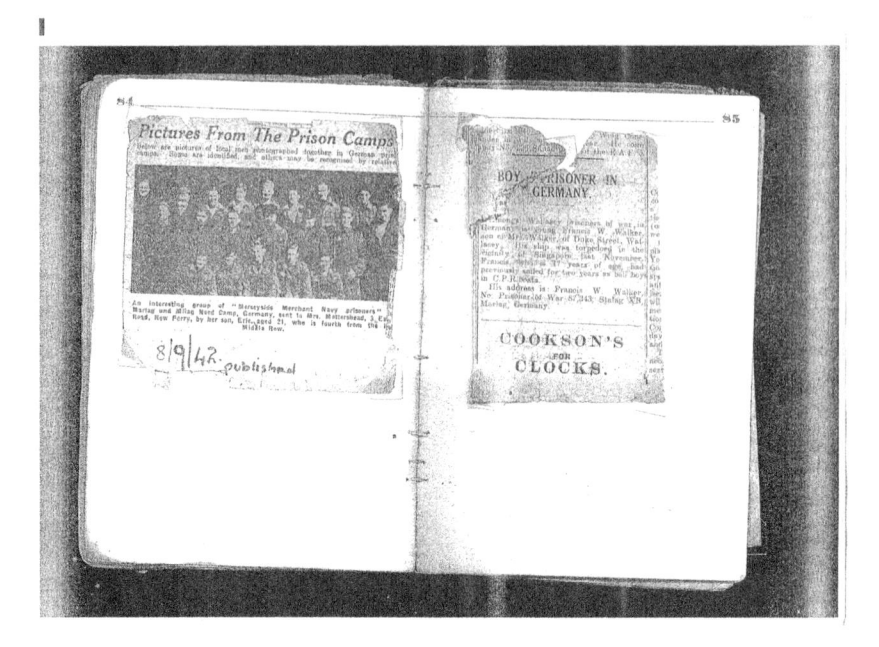

We made it in the press at home from time to time. *Newspapers unknown .Extract from the Frank Walker war diary, courtesy of the estate of Frank Walker* 'There was one about me in 1942, and that gave my spirit a big lift.'

* * *

'One of the blokes here, Tim Mc Coy, lived in Curate Road over by Anfield. He'd been captured at Crete from the 'Logician', a Harrison's of Liverpool boat. Tim was a bit of a minstrel and played guitar. He put to music a poem another bloke we knew as 'Snowy' had written for his fiancée. It's a shockin' shame really, that for all the time we were in that camp together, knowing just about all there is to know about one another in no-time at all, I don't think I ever got to know Snowy's proper name.

Anyway, Snowy and his girlfriend had planned their wedding for his next leave, but his ship got itself sunk in the Atlantic and he ended up in here with us instead of standing alongside her at the altar in North London. It's a lovely poem that they turned into song. 'Until the dawn, my love.' [editor's note: Snowy's poem is reproduced in the end pages of this book]'Quite a bunch of us were here from Merseyside and it was always uplifting for us to know we were not forgotten back home.

94

STAR'S VE DAY PRIZE WINNER

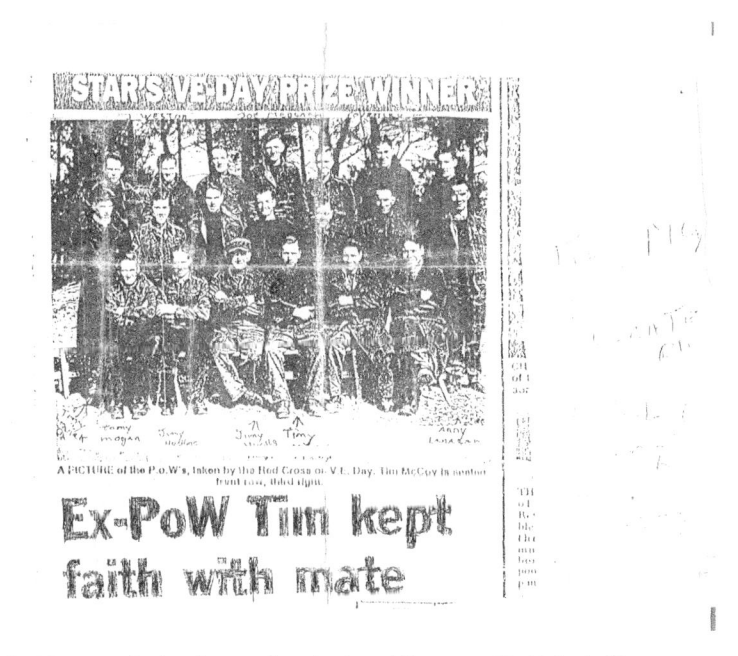

A PICTURE of the P.o.W's, taken by the Red Cross on V.E. Day. Tim McCoy is seated front row, third right.

Ex-PoW Tim kept faith with mate

Applied for permission from editor Andrew Kilmurray, St. Helen's Star 11/11/23

'Our folks sent us local press clippings of articles published about us that gave us heart.

'As it happened, Snowy's fiancée lived in North London and he'd lost contact with her while he'd been a POW. London took its fair share of bombs during the blitz and he thought she must have been bombed out. Anyway, one of the first things he did when he got out of Milag was to seek her out.

'To his great joy he found the house still intact at her old address, and a neighbour in the street told him she still lived there. With his heart racing he banged on the door and couldn't keep his feet still while he waited for it to open.

'His girlfriend opened the door on him, full of surprise she was, more so because she was holding a babe in her arms. Then from the room behind her he heard a bloke with a deep bass voice calling out: "Who's that at the door, love?"

Snowy went away to drown his sorrows, but the poem wasn't wasted. Tim McCoy had it properly set to music with his tune. They took it

95

over to a musician in Rodney Street, Liverpool, who arranged it properly and they recorded the song–'Until the Dawn, My Love.'

It was no good now for his old girl friend so they dedicated it to all ex-POW's and their wives and girlfriends. Nice One Tim and Snowy!'

* * *

"One of the lads in the camp we called Tarkieva, or The Japanese Scouser. I found out later his real name was Kenji Takaki. He always said, and he said it every bloomin' day, that once the war was over, he'd become a film star.

His family had originally come over from Japan and he grew up on Merseyside. We used to rib him rotten about his ambition. It was like him saying he was gonna win on Vernons Pools, but the last laugh was on us, because after he got home, he actually made it in the movies. You can see him, working with Virginia McKenna in 'A Town Like Alice', and with Alec Guinness in 'The Bridge on the River Kwai' and quite a few more too. That's him on the centre row left of an article published in Mersey Mart some years later.'

Kenji Takaki, the 'Japanese Scouser' *Reproduced by kind permission of the editor of the Liverpool Echo, successors to Mersey Mart.*

* * *

'Barbary Coast'6 *Courtesy of the estate of Frank Walker*

'This picture is of us doing one of our shows. Stan Hugill wrote this one. When I asked him afterwards what he had thought of the show. He just pursed his lips, waved his hand around his head and said, 'It was a bit west of north-west for my liking': all very nautical, but that was our Stan. I guess he couldn't forget he'd been on the wheel when *Automedon* bought it and he ended up the only one on the Bridge who had survived its shelling.

* * *

'I was buddies with almost everyone at Milag, but Les Lace from Barrow became a bit of a special buddy to me. Les was quite a good artist, and we would sit and chat while he sketched: that's if he could find anything to sketch on. Only after he came to Milag did he find out he had a talent for cartooning. The below is one he did 'specially for me.'

Courtesy of the estate of Frank Walker.

* * *

Toward the end of our time at Milag the Jerry planes flying over us became fewer in number, and the ones from the RAF and the USAAF more frequent.

'They not only dropped bombs on the docks, factories and warehouses, but took extra risks to scatter leaflets over the residential areas as well, just to tell the German people the truth about what was really going on.

'I never knew if it did any good or not, it seemed to us that the German civilians were every bit as much in captivity of sorts as we were.

> DER ANFANG VOM ENDE

These leaflets were dropped from our planes to keep the German informed of the truth

Courtesy of the estate of Frank Walker

'The day came when it looked like we would actually survive this rotten war and be free men again. We started looking forward to going home to our families and having a proper pint, and propping up the bar in a proper pub once more.

'I got ready for the day when I'd get out of here by sketching a special page in my diary. All I'd have left to do when the last day came around would be for me to write in at its top the total number of days I had been held in captivity.'

'For contrast with our spirits on our last days there, this page is a reminder of how it was, and how we felt and thought back in '41 and '42. We had nothing but uncertainty to look forward to then, day after day after blinkin' day.'

99

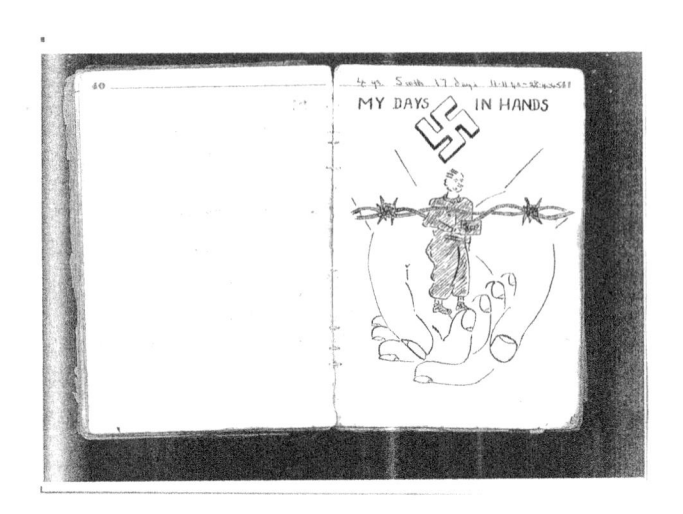

Day's Done in Milag *Courtesy of the estate of Frank Walker.*

Day after day of mind-numbing uncertainty... *Courtesy of the estate of Frank Walker*

'That downbeat attitude changed once we knew our own troops were getting ever closer to us. We even had news bulletins from the BBC because we had guys who could make up little radio sets out of scrap bits and pieces and silver paper.

Radio sets were strictly verboten, so these ones had to be made and used in secret, and then they had to be hidden away. It struck me then about how much knowledge and skills outside of seafaring people among us in the camp actually possessed. They seemed to be able to rig or make anything out of nothing but rubbish.

'By now we knew Monty and the boys in khaki were on there way here for us. Only days left for us to do in here now. *'Come on the lads in bearskins'!'*

* * *

'Hitler and his Nazi gang had tried all sorts of stunts to keep themselves and their war from ending. They were by now running very short of manpower in Germany. As a consequence, they even tried a ruse to recruit some of us to fight for them in their army. Below is one of the recruiting posters they quite regularly circulated among us towards the end of the war.

'Believe it or believe it not, four of our lads actually took Hitler up on his invitation and went and joined his army.

'In a way, I understand why they did it, and I don't blame 'em for it. When you are at a deep low and you can see no future for yourself, that's when everything looks bleak and uncertain. It does make you do strange, even self-destructive things to break yourself out of that vicious spiral.

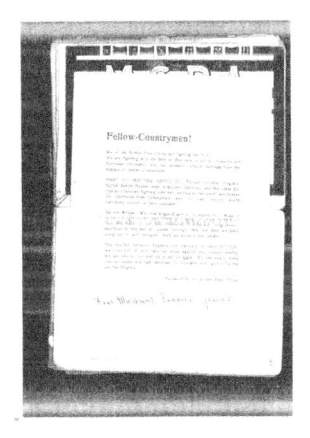

Courtesy of the estate of Frank Walker

'You have to be extra-strong to resist those harmful urges when they come over you–everybody got them from time to time. But only four of us gave away their whole future to get themselves free of where they were and from the horrors rolling around in their heads that were besieging them at that moment. I never did find out what became of them, or if they even survived the war. It would be the Devil's Luck for them to have ended up in a Soviet POW camp after what they had been through in Sandbostel and Milag.

Courtesy of the estate of Frank Walker

* * *

'Our camp came near to overcrowding near the end, and not all the residents were seafarers. There were about 8000 of us all told in Milag-Marlag by the last day of the war. I heard about half of that number were British seamen, 3,960 men in all. One day, I wondered how many ships could that many men crew? How many ships had been lost? I wrote a monument page to those lost ships to illuminate my war diary– it's actually a list of all the ships the blokes here were sailing on when they got 'emselves sunk by Jerry.

LIBERATION:

Guards Armoured Division with Scots and Welsh Guards at Milag-Marlag Nord. *Photographer not known, image provided courtesy of the estate of Frank Walker*

'Photo above is of Brigade of Guardsmen taken inside the camp on 29th April, but they didn't just drive in. Theirs turned out to be a hard fight to get inside, and just to get us out.

'On April 25th 1945 the air became electrified around the camp. Everybody believed this would be the last day for us at Milag. We knew the British army was close by and that it was coming for us. The signs of battle filled the air along with its smoke and noise. We heard on our makeshift radio sets that Bremen had already fallen.

'We learned that the 15th Panzer Grenadier Division, commanded by veteran General Eberhard Rodt had been handed the task of delaying the advance of the Allied troops towards Lubeck.

He positioned his stand with the Milag-Marlag camps standing between his troops and the oncoming allied forces of the Guards Armoured Division supported by the Second infantry battalions of the Scots and Welsh Guards.

103

'General Alan Adair commanded the Guards division. They were charged with advancing to cut off the 15th Panzer Division and to liberate the POW camps at Westertimke–where we were.

'We could hear the roar of battle and the scream of shells as The Guards started off at 0500, on the 26th April. They had a really difficult task ahead of them and had to fight against really strong opposition.

The boggy ground forced them to advance only along the road with their tanks and vehicles, and that had previously been cleverly land-mined by the enemy. They mined the road in a way that would allow the two leading tanks of a column to pass across unmolested, and then for the following tanks to explode the mines as they came over them. This would happen after a certain level of compaction in the road material by the first tanks going over them had occurred. This ensured that the ground supported less of the weight of those that followed. Their weight transferred directly to the sensors on the mines and up they went, and the tanks 'bought it', leaving the earlier couple isolated from support. The Welsh Guards alone lost nine tanks on that day.

'The Guards War Diary records the fighting as the strongest they had experienced since their arrival in Germany. The artillery exchanges continued from morning through to the evening, with the shells passing both ways over our heads across the Milag-Marlag camps, but, thank God we suffered no casualties from either of the barrages: lucky for us. We were more excited than scared by the bombardments, all of us were lying low, waiting and ready for our freedom.'

* * *

'Back at Sandbostel camp, just sixteen kilometers to our north we were later told by the Guardsmen that the sights, smells and condition of the inmates appalled even these hard-bitten warriors when they arrived to liberate that camp. They could not believe these skin-covered moving skeletons that they found were once civilised and educated people; or that human beings could abuse others in such an abominable way. The experience badly affected the Guardsmen.

'They told us of one German camp guard, who was so anxious to preserve his own skin when they arrived at the camp that he climbed a watchtower to wave a white flag at the oncoming Guardsmen. On the second wave of his flag they heard a sharp crack from a Lee-Enfield rifle and saw the man tumble to earth.

The Guards War Diary for the day records the incident, but the cursory investigation that followed found itself 'unable' to discover the identity of the Guardsman who had fired the shot. When we heard about it, we all thought that to be a right and proper close to the investigation, in the circumstances.

* * *

'The care and feeding of the POW's once he had freed them became a major concern to General Adair.

Extract from Bremer-zeitung- applied for 120323 *Courtesy of the estate of Frank Walker* © *Bremer Wilder Zeitung*

In their fighting retreat from the area, the Germans had left many vehicles behind that included mobile field kitchens. The Guards made immediate good use of these to prepare and give hot meals to us and to all and sundry; thereby freeing the general from his anxiety.'

'Only the strongly defended area around and nearby Kirchtimke needed to be overcome before the Guards could arrive at our main camp.

Around noontime, and under a white flag, General Rodt sent the Marlag camp commandant and his adjutant to ask the British commander for a ten-hour truce, ostensibly to allow the POW's in the camp to withdraw to safety from the battle zone through the Guards' lines.

'The British commanders stoutly rejected this request, for under the Geneva Convention POW's must not be moved. Moreover, such a lull in the fighting would better serve General Rodt, by giving him time to reorganise his troops that were somewhat scattered around at that moment in time.

'These envoys were not returned to the camp, however, they were held by the Guards as POW's. Kapitan Rugge and Leutnant Hauken were both naval officers, neither of whom bore any relationship to Kapitan Rogge of *Atlantis*. And, at this point, I'm all done and I'll hand you back to the bloke who's doing this book for me to let him finish things off. Ta-ra!'

* * *

As Frank said, the Guards were having a tough time getting into the camp. By 6.30 in the evening the fighting around Kirchtimke came to an end and the camp liberated by the Scots and Welsh Guards. After nearly five years of being constrained by barbed wire, Frank and his fellow inmates shook hands with each other as freemen once again.

The picture of the Milag-Marlag Nord camp entrance was taken on liberation day, 27th April 1945. The gates are held wide open and the men are milling around waiting to hear what will happen next–and when will they be going home?

Liberation Day at Milag-Marlag Nord © Imperial War Museum (BU 3 4835)

Frank is somewhere in this picture. To help you find him in the throng, he's the one wearing these POW dog tags:

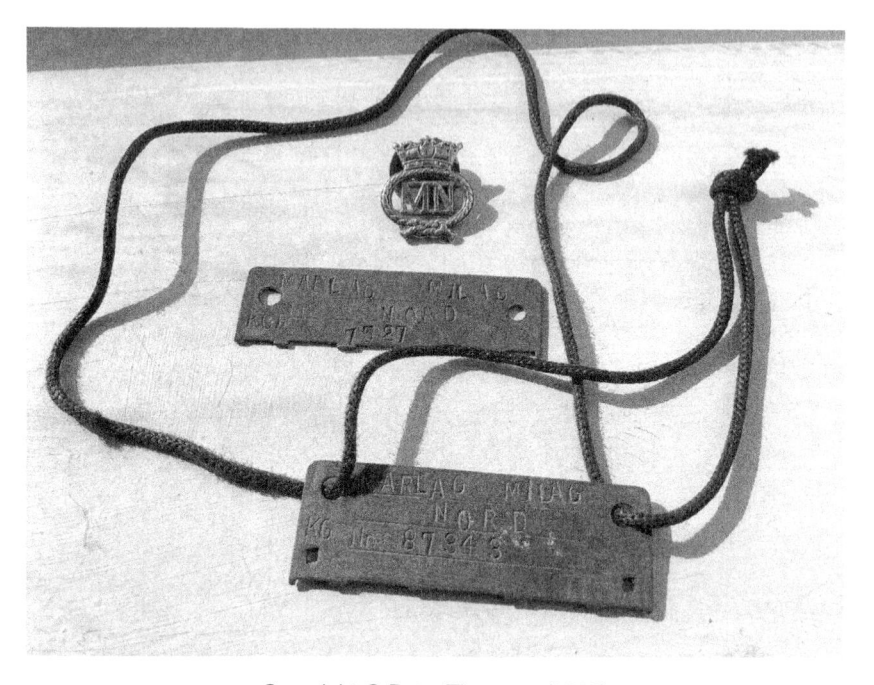

Copyright © Peter Thomson (2023)

After five wasted years of suffering terror, privation, starvation, intimidation, incarceration and uncertainty, the hardship and fear had come to an end for Frank, and the other inmates of Milag-Marlag Nord.

But gaining freedom for Frank and his fellow internees came at a heavy price. Four Guardsmen had perished on that day, and more still had been wounded. The tragic misfortune that befell one of these fallen Guardsmen is heard as the most moving story of all of those who perished or suffered in the battle that day.

* * *

Guardsman Gregory McKeand of the 2nd Battalion Scots Guards had been in action with his unit since 1940. He had served and fought with his regiment in the Home Defence, in North Africa, Sicily, Italy and Germany. He died that day in a land-mine explosion on the road just outside of the main gates to Milag camp.

It is especially poignant and ironic for him to have died on that day having gone through so much fighting and having survived its outcomes over the previous five years.

It is even more touching because this day happened also to be the last day the Scot's Guards were called upon to engage in active service against Nazi controlled forces in the Second World War. For the Guardsmen who had survived this day the fears of death or injury in combat loomed no more.

Gregory lies beside his comrades who fell with him in the Battle for Westertimke. They lie at peace together in nearby Becklingen Military Cemetery.

They provide us all with a stark reminder that the fight for 'Freedom from Tyranny' always comes at a heavy price for some.

Becklingen Military Cemetery. *Reproduced by kind permission of the Commonwealth War Graves Commission*

LEST WE FORGET!

RETURN TO SEA:

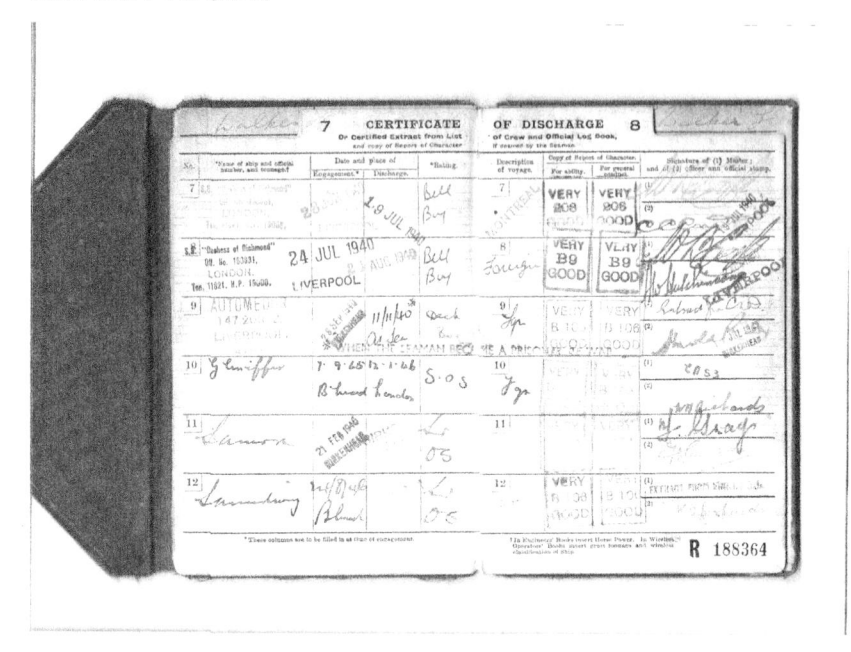

Frank's Discharge 'A' Book, showing 'Gleniffer' as his first ship on return to sea life *Courtesy of the estate of Frank Walker*

Frank wasted little time before deciding what he would do with his life on being hit with the sudden realisation that freedom came with a need for him to earn his own living. It did not take him long to decide to return to sea, and we can see here in his discharge book that on the 7th September 1945 he joined Glen Lines passenger-cargo vessel, *'Gleniffer'*. It was just four short months after his release from Milag. A major difference being that he now had an abode and a mother in Colville Road, New Brighton to come home to at the end of each trip.

Frank soon settled back into sea-life, and into the deck department, where he rapidly gained the essential skills, experience and abilities to bring him a successful life at sea. When he finally 'swallowed the anchor' and retired from seafaring it was as a highly regarded Bosun with the famous Blue Funnel line.

Frank had spent his adolescent years confined behind barbed wire in Germany. His twenty-first birthday had passed already when he came home from his incarceration in Europe.

In 1945, twenty-one was the official age of adulthood in Britain. Men of his age were getting married and settling down in their own homes. Frank had missed so much of his youth in prison that it prompted him to set up home for himself as a catch-up on his wasted years. He very soon met and married a German girl, putting his camp-acquired foreign language abilities to good use, but it didn't work out for them, and they soon split amicably and went their separate ways.

Fate had always intended Frank and Vera to be together. Although they were a few years apart in age, they had grown up around each other and had always harboured a soft spot the one for the other and enjoyed an amicable friendship. Vera had married while Frank languished in Germany. However, it proved not to be a happy marriage; and its failure had nothing to do with Frank in any way.

Vera and Frank had remained in touch through proper channels, and with her husband's knowledge and connivance. After his release, when on his leaves from sea, Frank would occasionally borrow their caravan that they kept on the coast. But when Vera's marriage failed and they finally divorced, neither Frank nor Vera had far to look to find a soul mate with whom to share their remaining years together.

They were married in 1977 and lived happily together until Frank quietly 'slipped his cable' in 2008 after thirty-one years of happy and contented marriage.

Gemeinde Sandbostel
Der Bürgermeister

Gemeinde Sandbostel, Beverner Str. 1 a, 27446 Sandbostel

Hausadresse:
Sandbostel
Beverner Str. 1a

Frank Walker
Vera Walker
Liverpool

Telefon Bürgermeister:
(04284) 930713
Internet: www.selsingen.de

Telefon Verwaltung:
(04284) 930713

Ihr Zeichen, Ihre Nachricht	Bitte bei Antwort angeben: Mein Zeichen	Auskunft erteilt	Datum
		Herr Schroeder	18.04.2005

Gedenkfeier zum 60. Jahrestag der Befreiung des ehm. Kriegsgefangenenlagers Sandbostel
Einladung der Ehrengäste zum Abendempfang

Sehr geehrter Herr Walker,
Sehr geehrte Frau Walker,

zum Abendempfang der Ehrengäste aus Anlass der Gedenkfeier zum 60. Jahrestag der Befreiung des ehm. Kriegsgefangenenlagers Sandbostel am

<u>**Donnerstag, dem 28. April 2005, 19.30 Uhr,**</u>

in der Gaststätte „ *Zum grünen Jäger*" in Sandbostel, möchte ich Sie herzlich einladen.

Nach dem offiziellen Begrüßungsprogramm und Ansprachen ist ein gemeinsames Abendessen vorgesehen.

Mit freundlichem Gruß

(Clement-Volker Poppe)
Bürgermeister

Bankverbindungen:

Frank's Invitation to Sandbostel 2005 *Grateful thanks to the Burgermeister of Sandbostel, Courtesy of the estate of Frank Walker*

REUNION:

But Germany hadn't quite finished with Frank after his release in 1945. Sixty years after having left Westertimke, with its memories of oppression and privation largely behind him, he and his wife, along with other surviving ex-captives, received an invitation from the Burgermeister of Bremen to return to Sandbostel for a celebration of mutual forgiveness.

The motivating German principle being a series of events over two days between 27th and 29th April 2005 on the keynote theme of:

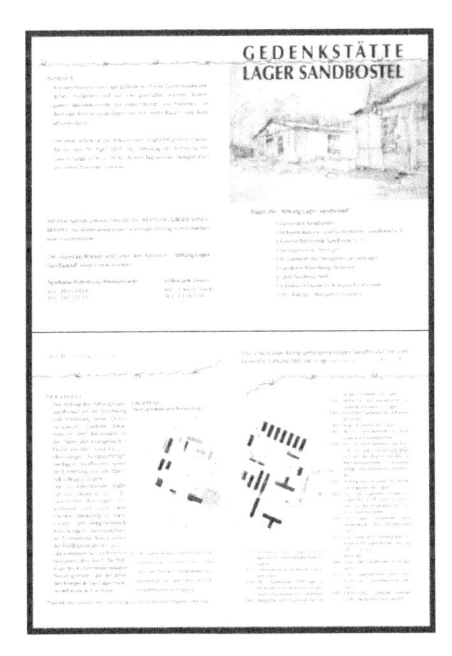

'We forgive and ask to be forgiven.'

The Town's Reunion Programme Grateful thanks to the Bergermeister of Sandbostel and to the estate of Frank Walker

Frank and Vera readily accepted the invitation and its theme of forgiveness.

Frank said he made the journey in more comfortable railway stock than he had enjoyed the first time he had travelled to Bremervorde station, sixty-five years previously.

The events were well arranged and enjoyable, but none more so for Frank than meeting up with his old comrades with whom he had shared those Hitler wasted years of his youth.

The all too familiar surroundings brought home to Frank another truth, that the loss of youth is yet another foul and heavy price of war.

Old Comrades Reunited *Thanks to Nautilus Telegraph and courtesy the estate of Frank Walker.*

The men stood close together, but in silence, each with his private thoughts and memories as they looked upon the sole remaining hut from their time before.

And each remarked over a large chuckle that there was no sign of 'Smelly-Nelly', she having suffered the hellfire of cremation many years before.

The Last Remaining POW Hut *Thanks to Nautilus International, courtesy of the estate of Frank Walker.*

* * *

Snowy's poem made into Tim McCoy's song, 'Until the Dawn, My Love,' came into their minds and onto their lips as a memorial to Snowy, Tim and those of their number who had crossed the bar and were no more. Mersey Mart had published their story and the song in the local Merseyside press in 1970.

Sandbostel Memorial Plaque Courtesy of Nautilus International and the Frank Walker estate

There followed a service and the unveiling of a memorial plaque to those who had been imprisoned and had suffered at Milag, and especially for those who had died there in the service of their country. A solemn moment for all, and as Frank stood there and considered the vast numbers of Merchant Seamen who had perished because of the war; a powerful thought passed through his mind:

"Had I not been a POW from 1940, my own chances of survival until 1945 would have been low."

MARINERS PARK:

Mariners' Park War Memorial Photo courtesy of Captain Peter Thomson

In his later years in retirement, Frank proved himself to be a generous, happy go lucky ex-Bosun who enjoyed a pint with his friends and with whom he shared his life stories.

Vera assured me they were always stories of the jocular kind, but he rarely, if ever, spoke of his time as a POW.

From its outset, life for Frank had never been easy, but in later, more mature life he enjoyed the love and companionship of the love of his life for the rest of his days in their home together, on the 'old salts' complex at Mariners Park, beside the Mersey.

Of his trials and tribulations let us in the next picture give Frank the last word on them, and as he said it in his war diary:

The end of the old life and the beginning of the new! *Courtesy of the estate of Frank Walker*

THE END:

Frank William Walker *Photo courtesy of Nautilus Telegraph and the estate of Frank Walker* Dear Reader, I give you the memory of Frank William Walker. A Good Lad!

Captain Thomson wishes to thank all those who have provided material by way of anecdotes, memories, photographs and artefacts to make this talk and publication possible. While he has made considerable efforts to observe the rights of copyright, he has unfortunately not been successful in locating all parties who may hold rights to some pictures included in this talk. In his pursuit to provide historical accuracy and completeness, Captain Thomson declares he had no intention to infringe those rights and has made many attempts to contact those who might be copyright holders. Should the inclusion of any material in this publication offend a person's proven rights, Captain Thomson will immediately take down any material that causes any such offense.

ABOUT THE BOOK:

Hidden away from the busy urban mass of modern Wallasey one discovers Mariners' Park. Situated on the Wirral banks of the Mersey, facing Liverpool's iconic waterfront, this sixteen acre green oasis has been home to come-ashore seafarers since 1800.

One cannot fail to notice the twenty-seven memorial benches, each one strategically placed at vantage points and all bearing the name in remembrance of a past resident, all but two having lived for what is universally recognised as a full lifespan. It is a home predominantly, therefore, for the more mature seafarers and their spouses.

I do believe it was Scottish comedian, Billy Connolly, who made the old African proverb better known when he said: 'When you look at an elderly person, you are not looking at withered skin, buckled legs and swollen joints; you are looking at a library that will be lost when they are gone.' Or similar words.

People who have lived a full and varied life will abound with stories to tell of their times and experiences– none more so than seafarers whose skillfulness in 'spinning a yarn' or 'swinging a lamp', as seafarers define storytelling, is legendary.

This book is about the man behind one of those memorial benches. A bench dedicated to the memory of Frank William Walker, a former resident of the Park, who has since 'crossed the bar' and gone to his rest.

The author is himself a former seafarer and presently resident at Mariners' Park. He produced two speeches on Frank's life, collating the factual material left by Frank and enlarged and completed from other sources.

This is Frank's true story that follows and serves as another worthy memorial to a man who belonged to the world's 'Golden Generation', and which now belongs to the world.

If he were here today, Frank would hope you would enjoy reading about him, of his fellows and of their times, before, after and during their seafaring days, in a bleak period when the world had gone to war for the second time.

'UNTILL THE DAWN MY LOVE'

The Poem written by 'Snowy', for his fiancée

Until the dawn, my love,
How many moons will shine above
Until I make you mine, my love?
How many days will dawn?
Do many bluebirds fly, across the
Same old Summer sky?
How many lonely nights go by?
While I remain alone.

How many rivers will flow to the sea?
How many times will it rain?
How many dreams will you dream of me?
Darling, will we meet again?
Though Autumn leaves will fall
Upon the same old garden wall.
I know my lonely heart will call
Until the dawn, my Love.
Until the dawn, my Love.

Written by 'Snowy' between 1941-45 in Milag-Marlag Nord.
Set to music by Tim Mc Coy, of Anfield, Liverpool
All Rights Reserved

ACKNOWLEDGEMENTS

One of the greatest fears facing an author when writing one's thanks to those who have helped in the production of the work, is to have inadvertently left out an important collaborator from the named appreciations. I sense that dread swirling through my body as a I write to give out my thanks. Should I have left an important contributor unmentioned, please be assured it is unintentional and a mistake for which I humbly apologise and offer age and increasing infirmity as my paltry excuse.

Writing a book such as 'Frank's bench' is a team event, and teammates tend to fall into two camps: those who assist in the collection and discovery of information, and those who help to assemble it into a book. Some, like my dear neglected wife, Janet leave footprints in both camps.

This book would not have been possible without the wholehearted support of Mrs. Vera Walker, Frank's widow, and their family.

The enthusiasm and financial support I received from the officers and members of the Wirral branch of the Merchant Navy Association in their sponsorship of this project has made it possible to come to fruition.

Author and Liverpool Historian, David Hearn, has made a significant contribution to the finished book. It would have been a product of lesser quality without his sterling input.

Similarly, the support and encouragement by author Roger Cunliffe-Thompson through the darker, 'dog' moments that seem to afflict all authors periodically, is greatly appreciated.

Angela Stevens of Cat's Pyjamas Design for the excellent cover and internal layouts, plus her infinite patience. Bless you, Angela.

Help and support have also been gratefully received from:

The Liverpool Maritime Museum; The editor of The Liverpool Echo; The Imperial War Museum; The National Library of New Zealand; Commonwealth War Graves Commission; Alan (Hack) of Riot Squad- the wrestling journal; The London Science Museum; Bremer Wilder Zeitung; Nautilus International; St. Vincent's School, Liverpool,

William Bixler and all others who have contributed to this historical dissertation – including Frank, who lived through it!

ABOUT THE AUTHOR!

Peter Thomson has lived a rich and varied career as a world traveller having served at different times as a sailor, soldier and businessman.

He has worked in his own and other people's businesses in the UK and USA. He saw active service during his military career in Malaya, Borneo and Cyprus. During a tour of duty in Berlin before The Wall came down he served on the military guard in Spandau Prison where the three remaining Nazi war criminals—Hess, von Schirach and Speer were serving their respective sentences.

His great love being the sea, where he returned to command a wide variety of ship types. Everything, he says, from a small coaster to a very large crude tanker.

Peter is a people person; a fair-minded man for whom human injustice against fellow beings triggers his rage.

When he read the simple inscription on Frank's bench, just two words and two dates engraved in two short lines, he did so with feelings of disappointment that they said nothing at all about the man or his life. And that set him off to research 'Frank's bench'.

The lack of a capital 'B' for bench is not a typo, but an indication that the whole story is as yet untold. The Guards freed 3960 British seamen from that camp on April 26th 1945. Each of those men had a story to tell, a story yet to be uncovered.

He will be pleased to hear your comments, and especially if you have seafaring forbears who were imprisoned in Germany during the war. Please also leave a review on Amazon and Goodreads. You can contact Peter on:

1sthobnails@gmail.com
(for clarification: 'first hobnails)

Contemporary Fiction:

The Stopover Series:

The adventures of a British businessman in a backward facing plains town in Nebraska, just before the financial crash of 2008

1. A New Road

2. Potholes.

3. Divided Highways

4. Crossed Paths.

5. Dark Diversions

6. Tangled Business (for release in September 2023)

7. Trials and Tribulations (Work in progress April 2023)

Drive For Freedom:

A fictional trilogy based on true facts surrounding the explosion of the perfidious side of the dancing boy culture prevalent in the society before the return of the Taliban. And why it led to western military personnel being slaughtered in their secure strongholds by the people they were their to protect. ...And the spread of the insidious culture to Europe.

1. Dancing Boys

2. A Boy Without a Beard

3. An Enigmatic Smile

Maritime Biography:

1. Frank's bench.

facebook.com/www.facebook.com%3FPeter.G.Thomson